More Special Deliveries

Jewish Birth Stories of Faith and Inspiration

Edited by
SARAH GOLDSTEIN

A TARGUM PRESS Book

First published 2007
Copyright © 2007 by Sarah Goldstein
ISBN 978-1-56871-433-2

All rights reserved

No part of this publication may be translated, reproduced, stored in a retrieval system, or transmitted in any form or by any means, electronic, mechanical, photocopying, recording, or otherwise, without prior permission in writing from both the copyright holder and the publisher.

Published by:
TARGUM PRESS, INC.
22700 W. Eleven Mile Rd.
Southfield, MI 48034
E-mail: targum@netvision.net.il
Fax: 888-298-9992
www.targum.com

Distributed by:
FELDHEIM PUBLISHERS
202 Airport Executive Park
Nanuet, NY 10954
www.feldheim.com

Printing plates by Frank, Jerusalem
Printed in Israel by Chish

Hashem plants a magnificent and luscious garden. Therein He places two gardeners whose responsibility it is to watch, feed, water, cultivate, prune, nourish, and nurture the garden. In turn, the gardeners implore Hashem for the siyatta diShmaya to know the proper measure, the exact quantity, and the right timing for performing each task in order to produce a bountiful and healthy crop.

The garden represents the children. The gardeners are symbolic of the parents, who need to constantly search for the proper and most expedient methods to encourage healthy growth.

This dedication is in honor of all children and parents in the world. Most particularly, it is in honor of and in gratitude to our own devoted parents and our delicious children and their produce, our precious grandchildren.

We ask Hashem that we may see continued Yiddishe nachas from all of them.

Shmuel and Rochel Rochkind

*Dedicated in memory of
our mother and grandmother*

Maddie (Marilyn) Leventhal

מאירה לאה בת מיכאל ע״ה

A true Eim b'Yisrael

She was a Shifrah and Puah to klal Yisrael.

*May the inspiration provided by this book
grant her neshamah an aliyah to the greatest
heights of kedushah, taharah, shalom, and
simchah.*

*With love from her children,
Daniel, Joshua and Rachel, Gavriel and Divi,
and her grandchildren,
Yoni (Yochanan Mordechai) and Yechiel*

People need roots. No matter where you come from, your ancestors make up who are you. Even when they leave you, the leaving itself makes you who you are.

In loving memory of our grandparents:
Joe and Dolly Karp
Percy and Mary Klein

May their memories serve as a merit and a blessing for all of us.
Andrea Sher, Raoul Karp, and Tracy Karp

לעילוי נשמת

חיה אסתר בת זאב יהושע

Adele Taback

Who taught and assisted women to fulfill their mothering potential.

Disclaimer: The stories in this book are not meant to be taken as medical advice. Any medical information contained in them was added to clarify the story and should not be used as a general rule. Each woman and each birth are unique, and the reader is therefore advised to seek competent professional advice before attempting to follow any of the techniques mentioned in this book.

Some of the names in these stories have been changed to protect privacy. The stories, however, are accurate.

Contents

Acknowledgments 11
Introduction 13

A Long, Long Time Ago
The Horse and Buggy 19
Birth over Forty Years Ago 24
Fisher and the *Tzetel* 28
In the Merit of My Mother 31

The Third Key
Living Miracles 37
The Ripe Pomegranate 41
Two Plus Two Is Four 49

Mothering the Mother
Vacuums Are for Carpets 57
My Doula 61
From Water…to Water 65

A Fresh Outlook
Birth and the Dentist 73
Yoga: It's Not What You Think 78
On Childbirth and the Redemption 82
My Brother's Wedding 88

Waterfalls
Shabbos Surprise in Manchester 93

    Surprisingly Simple 96
    Nesting 100
    The Postponed Barbeque 105

Birth from Above
    The Right Way Up 113
    Right Decision, Wrong Reason 118
    Big Head Facing the Wrong Way. 123

A Second Chance
    Blue Skies 131
    I Can 142
    A Third Try 149

Another Way to Handle It
    Birth #11. 157
    Challenges. 161
    My New Sofa 173
    Above the Natural Order 178

Grandmom's Heart Revealed
    What If? 185
    Tikkun 187
    The Miami Induction. 190

It's Not the Real Me
    Bringing Home Joy. 197
    The Doctor Is In. 203

For Fathers by Fathers
    Men Are from Mars 213
    Out for Fresh Air 221
    And You Thought You Were Tired? 224

    Appendix A 229
    Appendix B 231
    Glossary. 233
    Glossary of Medical Terms 236

Acknowledgments

I want to start this book by thanking Hashem for giving me the time, energy, ideas, and a healthy family so that I can help women to help themselves on the journey to motherhood.

I also want to thank the following individuals for their help in bringing *More Special Deliveries* to light:

- All the women who submitted stories or let me write their stories while they were busy with their newborns.

- The Targum Press staff for their patience and expertise.

- The knowledgable and experienced homebirth midwives, who continue to swim against the tide.

- Henci Goer, author of *Obstetric Myths versus Research Realities* and *The Thinking Woman's Guide to a Better Birth*, whose tireless work analyzing the information included in this book added immeasurably to help women have a safe birth.

- Michal Finkelstein, CNM, author of *B'Sha'ah Tovah*

and the *Third Key* and good friend, for her medical advice and emotional support.

- DONA International, for their wonderful conferences which keep me on my toes, as well as my mentor, Penny Simkin, for her guidance and support.
- My friends and family, who helped with the typing of this book and various other aspects of getting it published, sometimes from six thousand miles away!

Introduction

At last, after loads of fun, hard work, and international phone calls, my second "baby" is born. Although I have never personally had a pregnancy go past the estimated due date, I can now certainly relate to the anticipation and extra patience that's needed at the end of the process!

Even before my first book, *Special Delivery*, went to print, *More Special Deliveries* was being conceived. There were more stories to write, of course. But more importantly, I felt that some of the births I was being told about could have had better outcomes had the medical caregivers acted according to evidence-based medicine and centuries-old wisdom and had the birthing mom been more informed. Therefore, this sequel includes research and information along with inspiration.

So many women view birth as something to endure, something to get through as quickly as possible, without any thought to the spiritual heights they can reach during these incredible moments. In this book, I hope to share with you the stories of women who did it differently, women who managed to tap into their inner strengths during this challenging time.

Becoming a mother takes self-sacrifice, a giving when you think you can't anymore. Pregnancy and birth is only the beginning of the process, helping us to develop the abilities that we will need throughout motherhood and to strengthen our *emunah* and self-confidence.

Although the thought of labor is frightening to many people, overcoming that fear can strengthen our *emunah* as Jewish women. Today, when we are constantly being distracted by the physical and material aspects of life, we tend to lose some of our connection to our Creator. Birth gives us a chance to bond with the One Above, who gives us the gift of life. When we say *Tehillim* or daven for others as we are being tested to our limits, we can bond to Him in a way we may have never yet been able to. Hashem wants our tears, our pleas, and our appreciation during this momentous time.

As Rav Shimshon Pincus, *zt"l*, says in his *Sefer Nefesh Chai* (#116), the reason why birth is painful is so that a mother will use this time to cry out that her baby be a holy Jew. When the cornerstone was being laid for the Yeshiva of Ponovezh, a story was told of Reb Chaim of Volozhin when the Voloshin Yeshiva was built it was not made out of cement but of tears. Torah and the fear of Heaven are created from tears. So too, Rav Pinkus says, at birth, this soul, which will bring more G-dliness down to the world, will be created from the tears of the birthing mother. And this baby's foundation, and his whole future, is based on the mother's cries. So it isn't the nurse or doctor one should cry to for pain medication, but the One who gives the pain, the Ribbono shel Olam.

The stories in this book, shared with me by friends, neighbors, and others around the world, are from first-time moms and moms of many. They are stories of natural births and cesareans, births at home and in the hospital. There are stories from grandmothers and even a section for fathers. I hope they will uplift and inspire you while providing guidance and strength as you birth a whole new world.

A Long, Long Time Ago

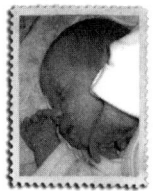

The Horse and Buggy
Chana

Our family had lived in Tripoli, Libya, for many years before Qaddafi came into power and we had to leave. For years we had lived peacefully side by side with our Arab neighbors, all of our children playing together as they grew up. Now, in the late sixties, the political climate had changed; Jews and non-Jews were nervous, and we knew we had to get out fast. Our only option was to go to Israel. We had always nurtured the dream of making aliyah, but it was so difficult to go. We had so much extended family — aunts, uncles, grandparents, and many cousins — whom we had to leave behind.

My father owned a small shop that sold a variety of household supplies: carpet beaters, washing basins, scrub boards. We lived very simple lives. Then, one night, my father told us that we had to get ready to leave — now! The very next morning we left by boat, making the journey to Israel, together with everyone in the family who was able to travel.

Along with us on the boat was the young man whom my parents had arranged for me to marry. I knew him from childhood and was happy with the idea. The details had been settled between our two families when I was only thirteen.

When we arrived in Israel, I was nearly seventeen. My father first took care of arranging accommodation; he settled the family in a small rural town in the Galilee. Then he looked for a rabbi to officiate at my wedding. There were about one hundred families living in our new village, ourselves included. We used horse-drawn carts to transport the vegetables we grew to the marketplace and to bring wood for our fireplaces in the winter. There were also a couple dozen bicycles that we rode on the dusty dirt roads, plus one old communal car that was used only for emergencies and to get to the monthly central council meetings.

My wedding was a simple, wonderfully joyous event. All the members of our community shared in our happiness. Two months later, I woke up feeling nauseous. My mother informed me that I was probably pregnant, and a bit of nausea was normal. She believed that women should rest during the first three months, to help ensure a healthy baby, so she prepared traditional teas for me and encouraged me to lie down every morning for a few hours. She cooked me savory stews and meat patties twice a day, pampering me and making sure I was well fed.

We didn't see the doctor right away. My mother wanted us to wait a while until I started to show. The doctor was an Arab from the nearby settlement who made weekly house calls. The nearest hospital, where I was supposed to give birth, was in Tiberias, normally a two-hour trip. My mother had had all of us at home, with her mother, her grandmother, and the midwife who was versed in the wisdom of the generations before. But instead of allowing me to do the same, she insisted that I give birth in a hospital, in the newest fashion. Births weren't better, safer, or easier there. Actually, I found out much later that many women who gave birth in hospitals ended up staying much longer than they planned to because they contracted infections that friends who had given birth at home did not seem to get.

The pregnancy went smoothly. My mother planned to come with me for the birth. The day I awoke with stomach cramps, the weather turned very cold and snow was forecast. As the labor pains started coming closer together, my mother said we should get ready to go. My doctor had visited the day before, so we knew we couldn't expect him to return to tell us if this was the real thing. I simply trusted my mother when she told me that the baby would be born that day.

My father went to borrow the communal car. We were granted permission to use it, but when my father tried to start the engine, it made a coughing sound, and then there was silence. Turning the key once again, he made another attempt. There was another sputter, and then the car died.

The pain was stronger now. We needed help. A neighbor came to see what was wrong and realized immediately that the engine was too cold and there was nothing that could be done. My father decided that our only alternative was to borrow a horse and buggy. I didn't know whether to laugh or cry when I saw the horse-drawn cart that was going to take me down the mountain to have my baby. But what choice did we have? As I climbed up, my coat caught on one of the wooden slats and my sleeve tore. I shivered from the cold.

Mother gave me a folded woolen blanket to sit on for padding, for the ride would be exceedingly bumpy. She wrapped her arms tightly around me, holding me close, and that was my only real comfort. I could hear her whispered, fervent prayers to G-d to get us safely to the hospital. My prayer was only that we arrive as swiftly as possible.

Winding around the hills of the Galilee, descending slowly down the mountain, it seemed that the ride would last forever. The wind was whipping through me and I was constantly shivering. The labor pains were coming frequently, but it was the bumps along the rocky road that distressed me far more than the freezing elements or the contractions. This wasn't smooth, paved asphalt — at every bump, I thought the baby would bounce right out!

The trip from our community to Tiberias could take two hours on a good day. Now we were taking forever. Bump. Bump. Bump!

Bump. Bump. Bump!

It seemed like a miracle when we finally arrived at the hospital, and I was shaking from the cold. A nurse immediately went to bring me a cup of steaming hot tea and then showed me into the labor room. Once we were there, she listened to the baby's heartbeat, checked my vital signs, and then decided we should be in a delivery room. She went to call a doctor.

I wasn't ready for this, for I'd barely recuperated from the long, traumatic trip. As though in a daze, I heard my mother saying, "It's all right; you'll see your baby soon!"

I remembered where I was and suddenly became aware of a strong feeling of great pressure. My mother was rubbing wine on my stomach, and the doctor who came in to join us announced that I could start to push. I didn't have to be told a second time (actually not even the first time).

Unbelievably, before I had time to even think about it, my little baby girl was in my arms. Her hair was black as the night and her wide, round, dark eyes peered up intently at me as if to say, "Thank G-d we made it!" I felt exactly the same way.

FYI...

Travel or riding over bumps in a road acts as a natural labor stimulator. It is important to keep moving during labor (even standing and swaying while being monitored) for the optimal descent of the fetus.

Birth over Forty Years Ago

Chelly Dorfman

Around 1960, natural childbirth slowly began to be in vogue, though most women were still being heavily medicated during childbirth. I had seen a movie about natural childbirth that was filmed in France, with a doctor discussing the benefits of this choice, for both mother and baby. I decided that when I was going to have a baby, this was the way I wanted to do it.

Soon after, when I became pregnant with my first child, my husband was recalled to the army reserves. He was stationed in Fort Lee, Virginia, which was over seven hours away. He only came home on weekends, so I went to childbirth classes alone.

When my due date arrived in March, it came and went; an uneventful week passing with no baby. The following weekend, I felt very slight twinges of something happening, and my husband drove me to the hospital that Saturday night. He was anxious lest I go into labor without him and he wouldn't be with me for the big event. He didn't want to miss any action. Though labor hadn't officially started, since it was a week past my due date, I was admitted to the hospital and slept over. In the morning, the doctor who examined me said I was beginning to stain, which, he told me, meant that birth would probably happen within the next twenty-four hours. The army gave my husband leave from his base, and we continued to stay in the hospital.

I was placed in a large room with women who had already had their babies. I walked around most of the day, with nothing much happening, and I even had visitors since it was no problem talking during that early stage. It was not until 5 p.m. that active labor began. I didn't know what contractions would feel like and was not prepared for the intensity of the pain. I got back into the hospital bed, but I didn't know where to put myself. I tried moving into different positions, but nothing seemed to help. It hurt so much and I didn't want to start panicking, but the pain was much worse than I'd expected! Why hadn't anyone explained to me more clearly what I would experience? I am sure that I would have been psychologically better prepared to cope.

I looked so distressed and my husband didn't know what to do (remember, he didn't go to the classes!), so finally, he ran out to call a nurse. She examined me and said I was ready to be moved into a labor room. Once there, I had the extremely unpleasant experience of listening to another woman screaming loudly at her unborn baby and her husband. The only positive result of this was to convince me that I certainly did not need to carry on like that.

When I was wheeled into the delivery room, my husband had to stay outside. Men were still not allowed to be present at the actual birth. So I turned to the nurse and told her that the pain was more than I had imagined and I wasn't coping with it.

"I don't think I can take it anymore!" I said.

"You took the birthing classes, didn't you?" she reminded me. "So you can do it!"

She proceeded to hold my hand and count with me through each contraction. She had a calm, reassuring presence, which was just what I needed. I didn't feel alone, and I was able to distract myself by counting and breathing, instead of focusing on the pain of the contractions. This helped give me back a feeling of control. The only words I uttered were, "*Oy gevalt!*"

With the support of this nurse, who acted like a labor coach, though that term was unheard of back then, I was able to relax and cope, and my labor went surprisingly fast. Four hours later, at 9:30 p.m., Sunday night, my baby was born. I then went through a phenomenal transition from overwhelming pain to exhilarating joy; such an upsurge of exultation that I felt like getting off the table and dancing! The nurse was so happy she kissed me.

I was given only a few short moments to bond with my baby before she was whisked away to the nursery and I was left alone in a cold room, with only a thin sheet to cover me. I was chilled and lonely and only saw my husband and baby again the next morning. By the time a doctor came to check me, I was run down and feverish from being cold so long. The diagnosis was impetigo, a highly contagious infection. As a result, the staff thoroughly discouraged me from nursing my infant, which made me very sad. My body was designed to nurse, and here I was giving bottles. There was virtually no support for breastfeeding, just as it was rare for a woman to be awake and have a natural birth without sedation. For my subsequent babies, I was more determined to nurse, and made contact on my own with La Leche League.

But the overall experience of birth as a tremendously wonderful event is something I've never forgotten. Knowing ahead of time that it will be painful, yet facing the challenge of overcoming and transcending the pain in order to welcome each new child, has been a high point in my life. I feel that being completely present and aware at the birth of one's baby sets a precedent for being aware and conscious of the child's future needs. Birth is the pivotal point of beginning for a whole lifetime of bonding together.

Over the years, when our four children asked about their births, I always tried to communicate this positive attitude of the wonder of it all, that the pain is worth it for the prize you get at the end, that exhilaration you experience in compensation when you finally hold your baby in your arms. They must have absorbed this message, for both my daughters and my daughters-in-law have had their babies only with midwives: a few in the hospital, several in birthing centers, and many at home!

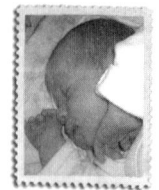

Fisher and the Tzetel

Miriam Fisher

I want to tell you about the birth of my daughter Ahuva Chana.

My son, David ("Dudu" Fisher, the singer), was born in 1951. Four years later I was expecting again, but the umbilical cord slipped out during the birth and I knew I was going to have a stillborn. The trauma was so great, I thought I would go out of my mind. Six months later I became pregnant again, and I was terrified of a recurrence. I went to Dr. Rabau, who was then working in the Assuta Hospital (it was 1957). He told me not to be afraid, because what had happened in the previous birth was a very rare occurrence. Still, I asked the doctor to be present at the birth. Although I had no money, and the expense of hiring the doctor was tremendous, I insisted.

The time of birth arrived, thank G-d. This time, I brought along a paper on which was written a blessing from the sixth Lubavitcher Rebbe, Reb Yosef Yitzchak Schneerson, *zt"l*. He had given it to my mother when she was experiencing a very difficult birth (me) thirty years before.

I arrived at the hospital at noon, with very slight bleeding. The midwife asked me to give a urine sample — but, once again, the worst happened. My waters broke and the umbilical cord came out. The nurse's face and her quick pace to the operating room confirmed what I already knew; the cord was my baby's oxygen supply, so the baby had to come out immediately. Three doctors scurried into the operating room. "Wait," I insisted, trying to place a small wallet, with the note inside, under my pillow.

"But it isn't sterile," said the nurse.

One of the doctors shouted, "What's the difference? Throw something sterile over it."

They operated immediately, even before I was completely knocked out, because, they told me, "We are afraid that the baby will suffocate." I probably passed out from the pain as the medication started to work. It was terrible, but all I could think was, *Will my baby be alive?*

Groggily awaking after many hours, I looked out the window to see that the bright sunlight had changed to a pitch black night. Eleven o'clock, ticked the clock on the wall. I turned toward the door as I heard the sound of approaching footsteps. Dr. Rabau came to see me and, after asking how I felt, said, "I am so curious about what was written on the little note that you asked to be placed under your head."

"You'll laugh at me," I told him.

"No, I won't," Dr. Rabau replied. "I'll tell you why. Before the operation, I told you that the heartbeat was very weak. In reality, it was nonexistent. No one spoke about it, but our glances to each other said it all. You told me, 'Operate, don't wait for the anesthesia. G-d will help me.' But we were sure your baby was no longer alive."

Then he continued, "I am an atheist and don't believe in anything, but from the moment I saw your healthy baby girl, I could not help believing in Divine providence."

I took out the blessing of the Lubavitcher Rebbe and gave it to him.

May the Rebbe always say good things about us in Heaven. Amen.

FYI...

A prolapsed umbilical cord (the baby's lifeline) occurs in 0.3-0.5 percent of births, requiring immediate delivery of the baby (within 7-10 minutes).

In the Merit of My Mother

Doris Ruchel

I am the fourth of five children, all of us girls. In 1942, in the period right before I was born, the peaceful life Jews had enjoyed in Tunisia for centuries was about to end. There were waves of unrest, and it became more and more uncomfortable for Jews to live among their Arab neighbors. When I was born, my parents decided that our family must relocate to France. My aunt and her family had already made the move several years before. My uncle was working as a tailor, and my aunt as a butcher.

A few weeks after I was born, my father left by boat for France. He stayed with his sister while he looked for work. He ended up joining his sister in the butcher shop, and immediately sent word for us to follow. Thank G-d, my grandmother was available to help as my mother packed up all our belongings. My grandmother couldn't bring herself to move away from the place her family had lived for generations, so, like many families, my parents had no choice but to leave her.

"Please come," they begged her many times.

"This is the only country I have ever known," she responded. "I am staying here with my friends. You make a new life for yourselves."

Though it was painfully hard for my mother to leave her own mother, she continued organizing herself and her four young children for the long journey ahead of us. Our tickets were already purchased and we had to leave right away, even though I, a three-month-old baby, was very sick with fever and an ear infection. The voyage took twenty-four hours, on a crowded and smelly old boat that swayed us across the Mediterranean, from Tunisia to France. It was very difficult for my mother, alone, but we knew we were on our way to our father and freedom.

Within a week after we arrived, my mother took me to see a doctor, since I was still not well. My mother was very concerned because I was so weak that I was not moving my legs. The doctor reassured her, "The trip was very hard for your baby, but she will get better and stronger with time."

He gave me immunizations, including the shot for polio, which I had not received before leaving Tunisia.

My mother had a lot of patience, and she nursed me to health for the following two months, blaming my continued weakness on the infection and the upheaval of our move. We were ten people living in the two-room home of my aunt and uncle, but we were able to manage despite the cramped quarters.

When I was four months old and still not better, my mother took me to a professor, who sent us straight to a hospital for tests. I was diagnosed with polio, which I had probably contracted before we even left Tunisia.

When my mother heard the news, she broke down

crying. Here she was, in an unfamiliar city, surrounded by strangers, in a large hospital with a doctor she didn't know. But, with courage, strength, and determination, she spent the next few years visiting me every day in the hospital, while I underwent rehabilitation. From the age of three until the age of eight, I had daily physiotherapy to keep my muscle tone as strong as possible. I could only go home on Shabbos and sometimes for holidays.

I endured eight operations during my childhood, including one to help even out the difference in length between my two legs.

When I was a teenager, the specialists involved with my treatment announced to my mother that I would never be able to have children. My mother did not accept this verdict. She proclaimed, "G-d makes miracles. We have faith." She turned to G-d, as the true Healer, and continued to pray.

I met my husband a few years later, in 1962, when I was twenty. He was not afraid to marry me because I had had polio. He was a nice, normal man who understood and accepted my situation because his own brother had a physical problem, as well.

A few months after our wedding, in the merit of my mother's heartfelt prayers, I became pregnant. The doctors insisted that I had no choice but to have a cesarean birth because of the paralysis of all my muscles from the waist down. They said my muscles would be ineffective for pushing out a baby.

My mother's response? "Let's try naturally."

The doctors could not fathom the crazy way she was talking, insisting that she was being ridiculously unrealistic. But they didn't understand simple faith. My mother was assertive, and they finally agreed to let me try.

At this time, my mother began lighting candles for

tzaddikim. She gave charity, prayed, and said *Tehillim* every day. She kept reminding me, "G-d makes miracles."

I was visiting my mother when my labor began. I was actually able to feel the contractions in my stomach. I wasn't sure what it was exactly. Maybe I had eaten something that wasn't good for me, I thought to myself. My mother, however, was sure that this was real labor and not indigestion. A few hours after we arrived in the hospital, without feeling any pain at all, my 5 pound, 4 ounce baby boy was born. Eight days later, we celebrated his bris, our tears flowing freely amidst the laughter, joy, and hugs.

Two years later, again with the emotional support and prayers from my mother, I gave birth to a beautiful daughter. The birth went smoothly and quickly. As a matter of fact, it was so uneventful, I wondered why there was a doctor and nurse in the room. I could have done this with no one around! Three years later, another daughter was born, also within a couple of hours.

After our third healthy child was born, the doctors warned us that another birth could put me in a wheelchair (until then I was able to walk with braces and crutches). This news frightened me. Immensely grateful to G-d for the three gifts He had already given us, it seemed best to heed the medical advice we were given and not take further risks.

In the merit of my mother's heartfelt prayers to the true Healer, I gave birth naturally to three beautiful children.

The Third Key

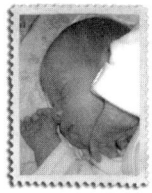

Living Miracles

Naomi Gold

I remember that Friday morning as the fateful day when a mysterious woman entered my life and then, soon after, disappeared — never to be seen again. In Jewish lore, there is the popular belief that Eliyahu HaNavi appears unexpectedly to be the bearer of good news. This woman was his female version. We were living at the time in a very small apartment in Katamon, an older neighborhood in Jerusalem. We'd been there for over two and a half years, and married more than four.

I was busy preparing for the approaching Shabbos when I heard a knock on the door. When I opened it, a rather large lady stood before me, dressed in a brown and beige smock, with a wide mauve kerchief covering her hair. Her brow was sweaty, as if she'd just run a marathon. Her bulky frame seemed to radiate an inner strength, and her eyes reflected a kind, concerned gentleness.

"Excuse me, do you have sugar?" she asked me.

"Yes, do you need some?" I replied.

"Thank you! And do you have bread?" the woman continued.

"Yes, of course, let me get it."

"One more thing — may I ask you for some coffee?"

These kind of encounters are not unusual in Jerusalem. I gazed at the face of this woman and felt that I could trust her implicitly. I cleared my throat and said, "Have you eaten? Would you like to come in and have some breakfast with a cup of coffee?"

"Oh, yes, I would like that very much," she gushed with obvious relief.

So I welcomed her in, cleared a place for her to sit at the kitchen table, and served her a meal. She seemed very pleased, grateful for my hospitality, and quite at home with herself and me.

When she finished eating, she stood up and looked around our tiny apartment, as though she was searching for something in particular.

Suddenly, she turned around, stared at me intently, and asked that probing question that I always dreaded.

"Do you have children?"

It was obvious from our furnishings (or lack thereof) that we did not. There were no toys, diapers, strollers, cribs, or other obvious signs of the presence of youngsters anywhere in our home. Though it pained me to say so, I answered her truthfully, "No."

At first she didn't answer. She continued to peer around, scrutinizing the pictures hanging on the walls and the books on the shelves.

Then she stopped, stood still, and said, quite emphatically in her lyrical Hebrew, "You will have children!"

Then she opened her purse and took out a small red thread. She told me to put it in a safe place in my handbag and carry it with me.

Not knowing what would happen now, I wasn't

prepared for her next words, "When you go to the *mikveh*, you must immerse seven times! And make sure to immerse in the *mikveh* of a bride, the same week that she has her wedding!" She spoke with confident authority.

I didn't know how to react.

At that specific moment in my life, I doubt my faith was as absolute as that of the woman standing before me. My husband and I had been undergoing fertility treatments for ages, and nothing seemed to be working. I was measuring my body temperature every day. I was taking an assortment of drugs, swallowing pills, and running to the doctor for late-night hormonal injections.

Fertility treatments were both time-consuming, aggravating, and — since they weren't working— depressing.

I stored away the words of my lady with the mauve kerchief and looked for an opportunity to fulfill her instructions. Synchronizing my cycle with that of an unknown bride, so that I could guarantee an immersion the same week as she, didn't materialize for months and months, which stretched into three and a half long years.

We were now married over eight years, and I was becoming more and more disillusioned, cynical...and almost hopeless. We made a decision to postpone treatments indefinitely.

Then one day, several months later, a relative suggested that all the mezuzos in our house should be checked and possibly changed. Removing them carefully from the doorposts of each room, I brought them to a qualified scribe for his expert perusal. The mezuzah that had hung on the doorway of our bedroom, he discovered, was *passul*, invalid. The problematic word was *v'shinantam* — the Hebrew word for "teach them thoroughly" — that comes before the word *l'vanecha*, "your children!"

Of course, we had the letters corrected. Strangely enough, this event coincided, the very next week, with my monthly visit to the *mikveh*. As usual, I asked the attendant, almost by rote, if a bride had been to the *mikveh* that week.

To my surprise, she answered, "Yes!"

I didn't know what to think. Should I entertain the possibility of being hopeful?

A month later, we were overwhelmed by the astonishing news that I was actually pregnant! Our first precious little miracle was born when I was thirty-seven!

This amazing fulfillment of my mysterious lady's words was repeated three and a half years later, when I again had the opportunity to immerse in a *mikveh* the same week as a bride. Just to be on the safe side, I made sure to have our mezuzos checked as well. I was forty when our second child was born.

Incredibly, one more child joined our family, when I was forty-four! Though their births were all by cesarean, that seemed like a very insignificant detail, considering the unexpected, awesome entrance our children made into our lives. Each one is a living miracle!

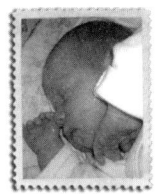

The Ripe Pomegranate

Noa Kaufman

The news that high-tech fertility treatment was our only option to have children came as a terrible shock. That was the verdict of the very first doctor we consulted, a year after we were married. Such drastic intervention, with powerful hormonal drugs and surgery, seemed more than distasteful: it seemed to go against the very essence of how we lived and approached life; trying to be so careful with what we ate and drank, consciously avoiding additives and known carcinogens.

Dismayed, we pushed off the additional testing that the doctor recommended. When I had bursts of willingness to seek other medical opinions, we saw more doctors and underwent more invasive tests, all with the same conclusion: IVF was our only option. But surely, I reasoned, G-d, who parted the Red Sea, could perform a miracle for us?

Yet each anniversary marked another year without children. I was wary of tampering with my body, afraid of exposure to Pergonal, Metrodine, Chorigon, and their potential side effects. How could I willingly expose myself to these chemical hormones to which no one could predict how I personally would react physically and emotionally? And a positive outcome wasn't even guaranteed!

How easily I remembered my vulnerability, seven years earlier, before undergoing the operation that had caused our problem. A team of physicians had entered my room on the seventeenth floor of Sloan Kettering Memorial Hospital, overlooking the East River. They had come to give me more details about the exploratory laparotomy that I would endure the next morning.

"Also, we will have a gynecological surgeon participate in the repositioning of your ovaries," explained one nurse.

"What?" I cried in alarm. "What are you talking about?"

"It is an important part of the procedure. Didn't anyone tell you?"

"No, nobody told me anything about it!" I sobbed, wanting to wake up and escape from this nightmare.

"In case we discover cancer cells in your abdomen, you will need radiation therapy on the lower half of your body. By moving your ovaries away from the lymph glands that would be exposed to treatment, we will be able to protect your ovaries from sterilization," she calmly explained.

I did not feel calm at all. The whole operation seemed unnecessary to me. Intuitively, I sensed that this highly treatable cancer had not spread beyond the lump in my neck and a tiny, almost imperceptible bump under my arm. But in the world of medicine, my intuitive feelings were not established facts that an oncologist could rely on to determine a course of treatment.

The next morning, half an hour before the operation, when I was already drowsy from a pre-op dose of Demerol, the gynecologic surgeon came to meet me.

"I heard that you were upset yesterday about the transposition of your ovaries," he began in a kind voice.

I was only eighteen. Marriage and family were not uppermost in my immediate life plans. Survival was first. I answered slowly, "I'm all right, I understand."

"So you are aware that tampering with your ovaries involves a risk? There is a chance that they may not work at all, but it is a chance we have to take, lest the radiation destroy them completely."

Shocked anew, I could not speak. There was no time to protest. For some mysterious reason, this whole experience was to be part of my life.

Looking back, I am grateful that I combined holistic approaches to healing with conventional radiation and surgery. I am sure that my wonderful oncologist was afraid that I was going to refuse treatment altogether. He had reassured me at the time that I would not have a problem becoming pregnant.

But that reassurance was given years ago, and now I was married and time was ticking by, with our hearts yearning and our arms empty.

A friend was foster parenting an infant whose fate was being decided in court. I became completely intrigued with the idea that we could become her parents. When my husband and I held her, we discovered how easily we could love her. We thought she was beautiful. One day my friend allowed us to help care for the baby. We changed her diapers, made her bottles, fed, held, burped, and soothed her. We cuddled her and talked to her. The very next day, we called the adoption agency handling her case and inquired about how to proceed in officially adopting her. They, of course, were obligated to inform us that there was already a six-year waiting list!

We were heartbroken by this news, but decided to continue the adoption process, attend meetings, and await "our turn."

Meanwhile, another year went by, a year of silently enduring monthly disappointments.

One way of coping with the quiet in our lives was to have Shabbos guests. Living in a thriving Jewish community near a college campus, we could easily welcome over a dozen students a week who had never experienced a taste of Shabbos in their entire lives. It was a privilege to be involved in answering their questions, and it gave us something to look forward to each week. It became an opportunity to share our values in a meaningful and life-promoting way. As it says in *Pirkei Avos*, "He who teaches Torah to his friend's son, it is as though he gave birth to him."

Another teaching that brought hope and comfort to us was the idea that a husband and wife, with the right *kavanah*, could create "spiritual children" whom we would meet in Gan Eden after 120 years.

Eventually I was persuaded by a friend to join a small infertility support group. There I met other women dealing with the same issues. In a community that was totally child focused, it was vital for me not to feel alone. One woman shared with me the *segulah* of saying *Tefillas Chanah* after candle lighting. The Gemara in *Berachos* records her words: "Master of the Universe, of everything that You have created in a woman, You have not created anything for naught. Eyes to see, ears to hear, a nose to smell, a mouth to speak, hands to do work, legs to walk, breasts for nursing. Praised are You for putting breasts on my heart! Why should I not nurse with them? Give me a son, and I will nurse with them!"

Identifying with Chanah's yearning, as well as with that of our four matriarchs, gave me a connection to a historical process that many women had endured, survived, and eventually triumphed. Surely Hashem would answer our prayers.

We willingly investigated suggestions of *segulahs* or alternative practitioners that sounded reasonably respectable. For example, a visit to a well-known *rebbetzin* gave me a stronger connection to reciting *Tehillim*. She also emphasized that I should have special concentration during the blessing of "*Matir Assurim*" in *Shemoneh Esrei*. "May Hashem release you from the constraints of your situation!"

What was I waiting for? I still felt too fearful of IVF to seriously consider doing it, but really, deep inside, perhaps... I wondered if I was worried about the implications of actually becoming a mother? How long should I wait? We were given only one medical option...when would I be willing to take the plunge? I wondered what was I afraid of. I prayed for clarity.

A good friend who was aware of our situation invited me to accompany her to the birth of her fifth child. A month after witnessing this profoundly moving event, I told my husband that I felt emotionally ready to visit the IVF clinic to begin treatment. We could apply our knowledge of holistic methods to the IVF procedure. I read up on guided imagery, which I had used while coping with the cancer that had directly contributed to our current dilemma.

We hoped that our years of prayer for Hashem's compassion, being *kvatterim* at *brissim*, and numerous other *segulahs* we had done, as well as the collective prayers of many people on our behalf, would perhaps have added up to tip the scales in our favor. We contacted rabbis, both for the necessary halachic guidance through the maze of fertility questions and for their blessings for success. We asked people, particularly our parents, to pray for us. We felt surrounded by a supportive network of prayer.

I recalled the trip to Israel we had made one summer. We had visited the Children's Memorial at Yad VaShem Holocaust Museum. In the dark, amidst the reflections of a million tiny lights, as the names of one child after another were called out into the eerie stillness, I pleaded with G-d to send us just one *neshamah*.

When treatment began, I prayerfully visualized each step of the procedure, imaging what was happening within my body: the follicles slowly developing into ripe eggs; my ovaries being protected from overstimulation by cool, soothing waters; the eggs joyously being fertilized; and a heavenly light guiding and assisting the embryos as they were implanted into the welcoming tissue of my womb. I pictured everything in as much detail as possible: the tiny little capillaries connecting and supplying our babies with all the necessary, essential nutrients to help them grow into strong, vital human beings; the lining of my uterus thickening with a fervent exuberance to shelter her new charges; and G-d's constant presence supervising all functions.

There were four embryos at first. Even though a multiple pregnancy would be difficult, and possibly fraught with complications, how could I pray for only one baby, and not express concern for the other three potential lives? *Whatever You decide is good, Hashem, but You should know that I am willing to host everyone!*

The Ripe Pomegranate

The days between blood tests were agonizingly slow. I tried to remain calm and optimistic, keeping my mind and body as relaxed and tension-free as possible.

At last, the crucial beta-HCG blood test tentatively came back positive. Two days later, a repeat test of this vital beta-HCG confirmed that the numbers had increased. I was definitely pregnant! An ultrasound showed one embryo had implanted. Our joy was immense!

But we still had months to go, with the fear of miscarriage uppermost in my mind.

In an attempt to retain some autonomy, we decided to learn to do the daily progesterone shots at home for the following three months. It was too easy, with an entire team of doctors, nurses, technicians, surgeons, anesthesiologists, and assistants participating in the intimate details of our lives, to feel like a piece of public property. Now, instead of having to rush in and out of the nurse's office, I could rest at home in privacy, using that time in particular to relax and visualize myself and my husband in a flower-filled field of the Galilee, beside a crystal-clear running river. In my mind's eye, I saw us sitting beneath a pomegranate tree that drooped with the weight of full, ripe fruit. In this Edenic setting, we prayed for healthy children. A soft beam of light surrounded us, and when it receded back to the Heavens, we were surrounded by beautiful, cherubic babes.

I turned inward, becoming very private as I focused all my energy on maintaining this precious pregnancy for the full nine months.

I quit work. I rested. I ate nutritious meals and avoided anything deemed harmful or unhealthy. I drank raspberry and nettle herbal teas to strengthen my system. I worried and tried not to worry. I cried and prayed and prayed and cried. I continued my prayerful imagery, picturing the changes taking place within my body, the baby nurtured and growing well. When the forty weeks were complete, on my due date, my waters broke. With the assistance of a competent midwife, many hours later, our beautiful, healthy baby was born at home into our extremely grateful, welcoming arms.

FYI...

There are fertility support groups in many cities in the United States, Canada, England, and Israel. See www.atime.org, www.puah.org.il, and www.chanasprayer.org for more information, or contact the author through the editor at emgee@netvision.net.il.

Two Plus Two Is Four

D'vora Grossbaum

I got married the day before I turned thirty. Okay, not so bad. Not too young, not too old. I knew myself a bit. (Does one ever really know oneself? Whatever that American expression means.) Yes, I felt the biological time clock ticking, but thirty wasn't so old. There was still time to have a pretty large family (about seven seemed like a nice size). If I wanted to follow in my mother's footsteps, four children was definitely doable before the time clock ticked off. It's interesting how even people who follow a G-d-fearing lifestyle have these thoughts that we are in control.

I was married four months before I became pregnant. I was nervous and excited, but before I had time to settle into the "pregnant mode," I started bleeding. Okay, I'm an educated woman; I've read the literature. The chances and the odds to hold onto the pregnancy were still good, so, with lots of prayers and help from my husband and family (long distance as it was), I waited. I spent the next month in bed before I miscarried. I was sad and disappointed, cried a bit (okay, maybe more than a bit). But, at the same time I felt calm, and I was grateful that a first pregnancy after the age of thirty was possible. Relieved that I could get pregnant, I was ready for the next one!

Thank G-d, I had two lovely daughters one after the other, with just fifteen months between them. It was so much fun — nursing, changing diapers, reading stories, and juggling two little girls with working part time. In between children, we moved from the United States to Israel, where I also tried to learn Hebrew. My fourth pregnancy also crept up on us very quickly. There were to be eighteen months between daughter number two and child number three. I would have three children under the age of three — and all of this before Pesach. I was excited and scared. How was I to clean a very small, new-immigrants' apartment with three little children? And after a third cesarean? (I had my cesareans because my little chickadees were breech.)

Suddenly, in the thirty-second week, there was no heartbeat. But why? Where did it go? Wasn't it there the other day? I didn't understand what had happened. I was confused. I kept telling G-d, "I can get the apartment clean and ready for Pesach. Just give me back the baby." I wanted him or her. I was ready. To make matters worse, my husband was at the apartment with the girls, and I was at the hospital. I didn't want a cesarean and no baby.

"Please, don't operate," I cried.

The doctors watched me for a day or two and did test after test, and in the end performed a D and E. Sort of like a D and C but different.

I woke up to find a doctor and a nurse sitting by my

bed. I felt like I was urinating in the bed.

"Relax," I was told, "go back to sleep." And I did.

When I woke up the next time, the danger had passed, but I did notice that there was an IV in my neck. Later I was told that I had received twenty-three pints of plasma and blood over an eighteen-hour period in order to save my life.

Okay, this put things in perspective. I had lost a child, but my other children weren't left without a mother. My husband wasn't left without a wife. I was okay for the next couple of months. After all, Pesach was coming. I would say *shehechiyanu* with real *kavanah* this year. I was alive. Mixed feelings whirled through me daily. Some days I was happy to be alive; other days I didn't know what I was living for. *Where is my baby?* I would think as I watched everyone around me who had a new baby or was pregnant. Being a mother of two wasn't enough anymore. I felt adrift, alone, and useless. While everyone was thinking that I was so together, I really felt empty. I worked, played with the kids, performed acts of kindness, shopped, and did everything else that comes with normal life. I was okay. I was fine. I had it all together — but I didn't.

Eventually, my husband and I got hooked up to a support group of a few other couples in the same boat with a fantastic facilitator. We learned how to handle the disappointment, how to handle the pain, how to go on. We wrote a pamphlet together on stillbirth and neonatal loss. Both of these things helped a lot. I also began providing phone counseling to other women who were in the same position that I was. This really helped and is something that I am still doing.

During the next couple of years, though, I was to be pregnant more times than I thought possible. Statistically, 15–20 percent of pregnancies end in miscarriage.

I remember hearing a story of a simple man and woman who had no children. Every year, the man traveled for three days to his rebbe to get a blessing, but nothing changed. Finally, one year, his wife begged him to go again and get a blessing for a child, and he did. Within the year, the couple had a son. They danced and rejoiced and the man went back to thank his rebbe for making his wife so happy, so fulfilled.

Before the boy was weaned, by his second birthday, he died. The parents were devastated. The wife asked her husband to go back to the rebbe and ask him what happened.

The rebbe told the man a story of a king who had had a son. The prince learned about Judaism and decided to convert. He then spent the rest of his life learning Torah and became a great sage. When he died, Hashem told him that he could have one wish granted. The prince begged Hashem to let him be born to a Jewish woman who had observed all the laws of family purity. He wanted to be nursed by a truly G-d-fearing woman. That wish was granted. This couple were the parents.

I remember thinking, *Okay, I can live with that*. If there is some higher purpose for my getting pregnant and then miscarrying I could handle it. But could I? Could anyone become pregnant ten times in just seven years yet have only two children? I feel like I had spent years being pregnant, being certain that everything was okay, going for a routine checkups or ultrasounds only to be told, "There's no heartbeat," "There's an empty sack," or "When were you told you were pregnant? I see a pregnancy that's about six weeks smaller than the date you have written here."

During those years I think I heard every reason there

was...and still no baby. Yet at the start of every pregnancy I still believed that I would have a baby. Where did I get that faith from? Or was I just being stupid?

I don't think I was stupid at all; I really had turned it all over to G-d. I knew that I had to do my effort and I really believed that all would be fine.

My husband and I had all sorts of treatments to help the pregnancies, things I had never heard of before. Then, as I was nearing forty, I said, "That's it — two is a nice number. Some people don't have any."

I was ready to give up. But, being an observant Jew, I wanted to talk to a *rav* who was a doctor as well.

The *rav* looked at all the paperwork from the various doctors and hospitals, and then told us to come back in a week. At the next appointment, he gave us advice and a blessing. I will confess I wasn't sure I wanted that blessing. I wanted to stop trying to have more children. I wanted to be finished with this stage of my life and to live a life on a more even keel, with less hormonal influence. Alternatively, I wanted to have a baby.

I continued to give counseling over the phone to other people in the same situation and, in general, life was moving along smoothly.

Within the next three years, we were shocked to be blessed with two more children, a boy and a girl. When my daughter was born, my oldest comforted me by saying, "Don't worry, Mom, when Mashiach comes we'll have a really big family."

The road to having a family — large or small — can be very bumpy. There can be treatment, miscarriages, and stillbirths, and yet there is joy, happiness, and pleasure. Finding the balance between the stress and the pleasure takes work and faith. For us, giving and receiving support, a husband-wife getaway, massages, a good book, feeling productive and useful in other ways, were calming and helpful, too.

My emotions fluctuated between denial, guilt, and anger. All these are exacerbated by changes in hormonal levels. Sharing the loss with others provides support as well as ideas of how to move on.

FYI...

There are numerous individuals and organizations that offer assistance to people who have undergone the unfortunate situation of having a stillbirth or a neonatal death. See Appendix A for list of resources.

There are also two pamphlets available: *Miscarriage, Stillbirth, and Neonatal Death* by Shulamit Allon, Jeffrey Allon, and D'vora Grossbaum, and *Strength and Hope after Stillbirth* by Tracy Prisman.

Mothering the Mother

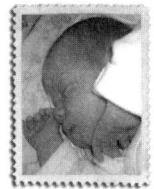

Vacuums Are for Carpets

Lieba Cohen

I met Sarah, my doula, during labor in the reception room of the hospital. Actually, we met by telephone the day before. "Hello, my name is Lieba. My regular doula, also Sarah, is away for three days at her sister's wedding. I never thought we wouldn't be together for this birth because we were together for my last one, which was my fifth."

"Yes, go on," was all I needed to hear because I was bursting with information I needed to share. My history came pouring out.

"My first birth was by cesarean. My baby was deemed 'too big,' 8 pounds, 4 ounces." The next three births were all with epidural. I was too scared to go through birth without it. At the end of each one I was too exhausted to push, so the babies were taken out by vacuum.

Vacuum — a word I never associated with birth. I grew up with three sisters, and we all shared weekly chores in the house. We took turns dusting the furniture, doing the laundry, washing the bathrooms, and vacuuming the carpets. Vacuuming was the job I had liked the least, but now it took on a whole new meaning. Taking dust off a carpet was one thing; pulling on my newborn's head was another. One of the birth reports gave the reason "mild shoulder dystocia." The other two: maternal exhaustion. All three babies weighed less than 7 pounds. The last birth, when I had decided to hire a doula, ended in a cesarean, just like the first. Again, "Too big, wasn't coming down" was what was written. We decided that I could birth small babies, with mechanical help, but anything over 7 pounds was just a "no go."

For my sixth birth, I turned to my friend, Miri, a childbirth educator. She had tried to help me before with advice I had trouble listening to. The main piece of advice was switch doctors. "Oh, come on. I've been with him through five births," I told her.

"Well, don't you think it's time for a change? Do you think it's so healthy for your babies to be suctioned into the world?"

Miri made sense. After speaking with my husband, I decided to meet a doctor Miri had recommended. This decision also meant changing hospitals. Our appointment was three days later.

Dr. Benjamin's office was simple, and so was he. No pretenses. He was straight, open, and to the point. The main rule that was laid down in that hospital was that it didn't allow Pitocin after two cesareans. And no vacuum — I would have to push this baby out myself. He listened to my hesitations and fears. We decided to hire him.

One month later, labor actually began. I coped nicely at home with the contractions, and I called Sarah, my doula, after arriving at the hospital. I was four centimeters open, and asking when I could get an epidural.

"Your best chance for a vaginal birth," Sarah said, "is to postpone the epidural for as long as possible, and let it partially wear off for pushing." I agreed to wait.

Walking around for well over an hour, squatting, hoola-hooping, and getting into a hot shower helped me cope. So did many of Sarah's pain relief techniques. I had never used aromatherapy or relaxation music before. I thought it was for less conservative people, but was quite surprised at the calming affect it had on me. The organic orange fragrance put me in the middle of an orange grove while I allowed the baby to descend.

"Okay, that's enough," I declared almost two hours later. "I want to be checked." I was five centimeters dilated, and even a bit more by the time the anesthesiologist came around to give me the epidural I was so dependent on. I wasn't trying to accomplish a birth without an epidural. My goal was a birth without interventions.

My body relaxed, opening up to full dilation in another two hours. When I started to push, I cried, "I can't. It hurts too much. I want more epidural." Dr. Benjamin gave me one-third of the top-up amount, thinking it would be just enough to take the edge off the pain without interfering with the pushing. (He regretted it later, saying that it prolonged the second stage by an hour, not a wise thing for a woman who has had two cesareans.) I still wasn't managing to bring the baby down low enough, although there was some progress. "Just do the cesarean," I said at last, giving up hope.

Sarah asked for the little-used squatting bar, which was in a closet somewhere. There I was, doing something new as I was on the verge of giving up. As I squatted to birth my baby, I felt a surge of strength, a renewed faith in my body. After four pushes in that position, the head came way down, and fifteen minutes later I pushed out our 7-pound, 10-ounce baby.

My baby's left hand was across his chest and next to his right ear, and this "compound presentation" had made the descent more difficult. The squatting opened up my pelvis wide enough to move the baby down. Finally, six births into my birthing career, I knew what it meant to give birth.

FYI...

As research continues to be compiled, we see that greater use of epidurals leads to more vacuum deliveries. This is due to failure of the fetus to engage in an optimal position, because the mother is lying on her back and the staff is too busy or lacks the patience to wait for labor to progress. Rather than using vacuums or forceps initially, a mother should be encouraged to move around and change positions.

My Doula

Nicole

I had a challenging first birth experience. Everything was fine until I went to the hospital. I went there too early. My husband and I had taken Bradley classes together, and we were certain he could advocate for me and support me entirely.

Well, I must admit, the level of pain shocked me. And I wasn't "progressing." The obstetrician on call broke my waters without asking me first. And I was told I had to stay in bed, tied to the fetal monitor. Not knowing any better, I didn't ask questions, and I certainly wasn't in a state of mind to advocate for myself. I wasn't able to move around at all, and the monitor was too tight, but I didn't know that. I couldn't manage the contractions. So I got an epidural. The finale was a "needed" episiotomy, which had to be repaired surgically, twice, a couple of months later.

Because of the epidural, I had trouble pushing well. The entire placenta did not come out. The obstetrician thought it looked okay, but it wasn't. I was sick, really sick; feeling so weak. The obstetrician didn't believe me when I told him the bleeding was too heavy. Three weeks later I needed a D and C. The same obstetrician then told me I had to pump and dump my milk because of the anesthesia. Well, Gabriella Hannah had an allergic reaction to the formula and then nipple confusion. From this experience I learned that it's very important to remember that your doctor is also a person who is (a) busy and (b) makes mistakes. If you feel something is wrong, speak up — again and again.

Fast-forward a few months. In desperation I discovered and joined La Leche League. With their help, the nursing and allergy problems were cleared up. Gabriella Hannah went on to nurse until age two years, eight months. She weaned herself while I was pregnant, and I became a LLL leader.

With my second child, I had a high-risk pregnancy. I was expecting twins at the outset, and we lost one at twelve weeks. For a long time the deceased twin's sac and placenta were right over my cervix. The perinatologist was very concerned that my body would reject the deceased twin, start bleeding, and threaten the other, growing baby.

By thirty-three weeks, just before we moved out of state, my risk category was downgraded to normal, plus "bears watching." The other sac was still there, but more out of the way. I did a tremendous amount of research, looking for a hospital and an obstetric practice that could handle my potentially risky situation, giving me latitude for a natural birth and a doula. Before the move, I searched the DONA (Doulas of North America) website, and interviewed doulas over the phone. I met with a few when we came to our new community to look for apartments. I chose one before we even moved there.

My doula was incredible. She was a friendly,

nonconfrontational person who was an invaluable help to my husband and me during the labor.

When I had to be induced a week after my due date because my blood pressure spiked, she was right there to help me through that agonizing choice. She massaged me, made me comfortable, talked to me, focused me, and helped me understand what was happening when I started to go into transition and began to shake. She was so friendly the nurses loved her and left me alone to do my thing, even with the Pitocin. She got me a longer lead for the machine so I could move around freely. She pushed on my back while I pushed, as my husband concentrated on gently talking to me, helping me focus.

When my Sophia Rose was born, she reminded the obstetrician that my husband wanted to stay involved and hold the baby soon after the birth. She also helped me to understand what was going on when Sophia Rose needed a little stimulation after the birth. She helped me get her started nursing and stayed until they moved me to the ward.

The end of the story: I gave birth without medical pain relief, despite being induced with Pitocin. I was the first person ever to give birth in that hospital backwards on the bed, kneeling. This was because of my doula and my husband. I needed them both, for different and complementary reasons.

A doula is not only there to be an ideological advocate for natural childbirth. She is also there to support the mother, the father, and the family — especially if things get complicated. That physical and emotional support is even more crucial for keeping the mother calm, centered, and free of a feeling that she did anything "wrong." No matter what your situation, even if you need a planned cesarean (like a friend of mine recently did, for a baby with complications), a doula is just there for the mother.

FYI..

According to Dr. John Kennell, one of the founders of the DONA (Doulas of North America) organization, "If a doula were a drug, it would be malpractice not to use it." At a DONA conference in 2000, Dr. Kennell said the following:

> Let me note that if I had told you today about a new medication or a new electronic device that would reduce problems of fetal asphyxia and lower pain medication use, reduce medical intervention and cesareans...cut [the length of] labor by 20 percent, and enhance mother-infant interaction after delivery, I expect that there would be a stampede to obtain this new medication or device in every obstetric unit in the United States, no matter what the cost. Just because the supportive companion [doula] makes good common sense does not decrease its importance.

Statistics on the benefits of doulas can be found in *The Doula Book* by Marshall, Kennell, and Klaus (Cambridge, MA: Perseus Publishers, 2002) and *The Doula Advantage* by Rachel Gurevich (Prima Publishers, 2003).

From Water...
to Water

Dalia Stone

I was sitting in the waiting room before an appointment with my midwife, already in my ninth month, when I happened to notice a pamphlet that discussed the advantages of something called "water birth." I read the whole thing, fascinated. Laboring in a pool and delivering while still in the water seemed very appealing, an idea that lent itself well to my desire to have a natural birth without painkillers.

When I met with my midwife, we discussed this option seriously, and she was very supportive. I had been through five long years of waiting for this precious child, and I wanted the birth to be a very special experience.

A few weeks later, the Monday morning right after Pesach, the distinct feeling of contractions awakened me. I was very excited. Immediately, I began putting into practice all that I had learned about breathing through each contraction, according to the Swiss antenatal method.

At some point, as the intensity of the pain increased, I decided to take a bath. The warm water was very relaxing, and it was with great reluctance that I finally got out, at my labor coach's insistence, to head for the hospital. Since I knew there was a Jacuzzi available to use there, it was easier to leave our home.

In the hospital, we entered a large room with pretty wallpaper, a bright and cheerful atmosphere, without one machine in sight. A midwife examined me, checked the baby's heartbeat, and declared that everything was fine. Then she started filling up the pool. The contractions were getting stronger and I couldn't wait to get into the water!

When it was finally ready, I slipped on a long T-shirt and climbed in. It was 4:30 p.m. by then. The warmth of the water enveloped me, my muscles relaxed considerably, and I had the comforting sensation of feeling more in control of the birthing process. It was easier to let go and totally relax, which definitely took the edge off the pain. I felt weightless, enjoying the buoyancy that made it easy to move into comfortable positions. There was a sense of timelessness about being there, surrounded by the protecting waters. The midwives and my labor coach hovered quietly at the edge of the pool, occasionally monitoring the baby with a waterproof monitor.

The room was quiet and I felt at peace and in total harmony with my body, flowing with the rise and fall of each contraction, completely absorbed with my breathing. The cocoon-like feeling in the pool made an enormous difference in my sense of privacy and my ability to relax. I could move about freely, but mostly I stayed in a kneeling position, supporting myself by grasping the edge of the pool. The midwives were there to guide me if I needed assistance, but mostly they left me alone, aware that I was coping, enjoying, reveling in the experience.

When I felt ready to push, I squatted, holding on to the sides of the pool. The room was utterly tranquil. As the moment of my child's birth approached, the rays of the descending sun, beaming through the slats of the window blinds, were the only light in the room. The next contraction came, I pushed, and my beautiful baby daughter entered the water. One of the midwives gently scooped her up and handed her to me.

It was 9 p.m. Lying there in my arms, she gazed up at me, with calm, alert eyes. I was absolutely awed by the amazing miracle of her birth. After five years of waiting, I was overwhelmed with feelings of love and gratitude to G-d for granting us this beautiful healthy baby. And I was full of thankfulness for the gentle way she was born.

FYI...

It is now commonly understood that babies born in water have built-in physiological reflexes that prevent inhalation of the water during a water birth. This is called the dive reflex. However, it is important that the right conditions be maintained to support this reflex and prevent premature stimulation of the breathing response.

In 1996, Dr. Paul Johnson, neonatal physiologist at the John Radcliffe Hospital, Oxford, published an important paper on the mechanisms that trigger breathing in newborns. As part of his detailed research into "practice breathing" by the fetus, he found that while the baby is in the uterus there are powerful mechanisms that prevent the aspiration of amniotic fluid into the lungs. These include (1) the presence of high levels of the hormone prostaglandin and (2) the warmth of the uterine environment.

Johnson noted that levels of prostaglandin rise in

the forty-eight hours before the onset of labor. Therefore, an intact placenta and umbilical cord circulation continue to inhibit breathing even after birth into water.

The temperature of the environment into which the baby is born is the main determinant of the arousal threshold of the fetus and, with it, the effectiveness of breathing. His paper explains that exposure, particularly of the baby's cheeks, nose, and mouth, to air that is at least one degree cooler than body temperature is the main stimulant to breathing in the newborn. As long as the water temperature is maintained at about body temperature, there is little risk that the baby will accidentally start to breath while under water.

In addition, a baby's highly tuned sense of taste triggers the larynx to close when the baby tastes fresh water, among other fluids. This reflex is designed primarily to prevent inhalation of fluid while feeding, but also serves to prevent aspiration in an underwater birth.

However, the comparative risks of birth in water to the baby were not known until 1999, when Ruth E. Gilbert and Pat A. Tookey of the Institute of Child Health, London, published an important an important study in the *British Medical Journal*. The study set out to estimate mortality and morbidity rates for babies delivered in water. These were compared with other sources of data providing similar estimates for babies delivered conventionally to low-risk women. Although just one piece in the emerging jigsaw of research, this study has provided significant reassurance about the safety of water births.

The study examined adverse outcomes that were reported between 1994 and 1996 from approximately four thousand water births. In the U.K., 1,500 consultant pediatricians were asked if they knew of cases where a baby died or was admitted to special care following labor or delivery in the water. The study revealed a similarity in rates of perinatal mortality and morbidity in babies born in water and babies born to low-risk women on land. This suggests that delivery in water does not substantially increase adverse perinatal outcomes.

None of the five perinatal deaths recorded among the water births was attributed to the delivery in water, and the rate of 1.2 deaths per 1,000 births was in keeping with the mortality rate for low-risk deliveries on land.

For further reference, see Paul Johnson, "Birth under Water: To Breathe or Not to Breathe," *British Journal* of Obstetrics, vol. 104, no. 1 (1996), and Ruth E. Gilbert and Pat A. Tookey, "Perinatal Mortality and Morbidity among Babies Delivered in Water," *British Medical Journal*, vol. 319, no. 7208 (Aug. 21, 1999).

A Fresh Outlook

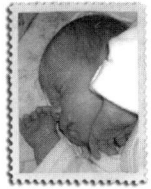

Birth and the Dentist

Aviva Yoselis

I hate the dentist. I don't mean personally. I'm sure he's a very nice man once you get to know him, but just the thought of visiting him fills me with dread. He's there for my own good, I often remind myself, as I trudge into his office gritting my teeth to face the worst. And it usually is.

Lately, though, I've discovered a good technique to relax myself and reduce some of my discomfort. I imagine what I'll do when the visit is over. I'll go home and cook an enormously tasty meal; my children and I will spend a leisurely afternoon in the park; or maybe I'll buy myself a coffee on the way home. The individual image isn't important; it's the "where I'll be after the appointment" that's essential.

I think this is how most of us get through labor. We go through those nine (okay, really ten) months of pregnancy, and we spend the last few thinking about what it's going to be like afterward. Sometimes this relaxes us, sometimes it stresses us, but we tend to view the labor not as an event in and of itself, but as a passage to that unknown beyond. I've been wondering to myself if there's a flaw in that somewhere. Is labor something that we need to dedicate much time and thought to, or is it really a matter of just making it through? Compared to ten months on one side and a lifetime on the other, it is a relatively short period of time in one's life. Maybe we just need to grit our teeth and go through it, much like sitting in the dentist's chair.

I hate pain. In every new dentist's chair in which I sit, I calmly explain that I've done natural childbirth, but I get nauseated even thinking about that little scrappy pick near my mouth. So could he please tell me everything that he's about to do before he does it, and use as many pain relievers as he can, starting with that foul-tasting cherry numbing material.

I ask myself, *What is my goal when sitting in the dentist's chair?* To see myself afterward, same person with an addition. After birth, I wonder, am I the same person just with an addition, or is something else at work?

My third birth, four months ago, seemed to be a bit of a spiritual experience, mostly for my midwife and my husband. For me, it was certainly uplifting and meaningful (more about that later), but I know it affected them in a deeper way. I went into this birth with much more mental readiness and previous knowledge than the first two. And I was in an environment where I knew and trusted all those present in the process.

But let me take a step back. Why am I even using the terms *meaningful* and *spiritual* in the same sentence as the word "labor"? Let me begin by saying that I didn't have an epidural for my first daughter's birth, mostly because I was more scared of the needle than I was of the contractions. I had known that I had wanted to try out labor "naturally," although in my naiveté, I had absolutely no idea of what that meant.

Birth and the Dentist

I arrived at the hospital at 12 a.m., two centimeters dilated. The nurse told me to start walking. "Try the stairs," she said. We did. For six and a half hours, with contractions every two minutes. By six-thirty in the morning, I was ready to have someone knock me out with a two-by-four, if only to just get it over with.

I can remember precisely when everything changed. I was in the shower, most likely for the fourth time, my husband nodding off outside in the hallway. I said to myself, *Okay, there has to be a way to make this go faster.* I remembered my imaging tricks that I had used when I was suffering from chronic pain. The single most important factor had been to let the positive light color wash through me and not to fight the pain.

Okay, I said to myself, *let's try to not fight the contraction when it comes.* I let all my muscles go, relaxed my jaw, and hoped for the best. The next contraction came as a huge wave and I had to use all my mental energy not to fight it. Then I felt this rush of energy that almost knocked me over. I felt as if my whole body were opening up. I had one more contraction like that, and was quickly rushed to the labor room by the midwife, who was afraid that I was going to deliver in the shower.

For my second birth, I thought I was prepared. I had my imaging tricks; I was ready to give myself over and let go. On the ride to Jerusalem in the ambulance, the midwife, who happens to be my friend, saw that I had progressed pretty quickly. "You know," she said, "this is a great time to pray. This is when the gates of Heaven are open, and Hashem hears your requests in a way that He doesn't every day."

I was surprised, to say the least. I hadn't ever considered this concept before.

So I prayed. I prayed for Hashem to cure my friend's

chronically ill child and to bring a new life to all those childless couples that I knew. The delivery did not go as quickly as I would have wanted; I was tired and worn out by the end, but I felt that something had changed within me. So I said, "Next time..."

In my third pregnancy, I said, I want the birth to be spiritual, connected. I want to feel Hashem's presence. A bit of a lofty goal when you're being held captive by an enormously strong muscle that's trying to squeeze a human being out of you.

My sister says that labor is all about surrender. Giving yourself over to that energy, whether you identify it as the life force in your body or the Supreme Being who manages the world. The letting go, the recognition that we, meaning our minds, are not in control of what's happening and that we must let that more powerful force have its way. That, to me, is the moment when true connection can come. When, somehow, we've let go enough and left ourselves open enough, so that Light can come down to us.

At this point, I'm sure you're saying, *Okay, if she thinks that I could have one uplifting thought during that whole painful process, she's obviously not mentally balanced.* No, I'm not saying that the birth was full of singing angels or halos of purple light flinging around the room. My labors are no forty-five minute affairs, and they are not easy. But I was able to put the fear at bay most of the time, and let go enough to feel that I was doing something special.

It was no longer about just getting through to the other side. It was about trying to connect upward during the most vulnerable moment in my life, and say, "I know You're there, and hey, I could really use Your help. In fact, so could we all. So how about it?"

I know that I have had other moments in my life when I have felt G-d's presence more strongly than in that delivery room. I would not define it as my most "spiritual moment." But I know that during that birth, my husband and my midwife saw something in my face that is not usually there. They were connected to that Light that was brought down. I was too within myself to feel it, but they saw me as a conduit, helping Hashem to bring my daughter into this world. That concept, of being a conduit for someone else outside of you, is why I think that labor isn't about making it through to the other side.

I am not actively participating in anything great as I sit in the dentist's chair. It's all about me and my discomfort (not to mention my cavity). Yes, labor is a brief moment in the grand scheme of life, both of the mother and the child. But we fool ourselves if we really think of it as fleeting and inconsequential.

Years later, I still have butterflies in my stomach every time I discuss my first birth, even though I consider it positively. Giving birth can be an overwhelming experience, but it is not fleeting, because it does affect how we view our children and ourselves forever.

There is so much potential within labor. We just need to learn how to access it.

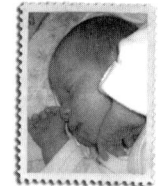

Yoga: It's Not What You Think

Meira Schneider-Atik

I'm a graduate student in clinical psychology. At the end of our first year, when we had to apply for internships for clinical fieldwork, I had a very difficult time getting a placement. Either I wouldn't hear back from a place or I was rejected outright. It was very frustrating, to say the least.

Finally, to my relief, I was offered an internship with the Cancer Support Network, a nonprofit group providing counseling and therapeutic activities for cancer patients, survivors, and their families.

I enjoyed the work at the Cancer Support Network very much. I liked my colleagues and my clients, and we were even allowed to participate in the Network's activities, as long as the patients got first priority.

One of these activities was yoga. Contrary to popular belief, yoga is not a bunch of people sitting cross-legged and chanting "ohm" — that's meditation. Instead, we did the form of yoga known as "Bikram." This consists of twenty-six postures and two breathing exercises that are designed to build strength, stamina, and flexibility, while working every single organ and tissue in the body. I was stretching muscles I didn't even know I had. In addition, the yoga made my former exercises (bike, treadmill, and weights) much easier.

I had read that yoga makes the body work more efficiently, so that people have an easier time with many functions, including conception. Plus, it's an ideal exercise for pregnant women; it keeps them in shape, making labor and delivery much easier. It helps the baby by increasing blood circulation and giving it more oxygen and nutrients.

A few months after I started my routine, I conceived. I had no complications during the pregnancy, only an occasional bout of morning sickness.

I did consider having a home birth with a midwife, but I felt better, stereotype or not, knowing I was under a doctor's care in a hospital. I must admit, I didn't do a lot of research, until it came to seeking a doctor. I found one who had a great record for uncomplicated pregnancies.

Our childbirth teacher told us that if the delivery is going normally, but occurs at a busy time in the hospital, the baby might be delivered by a resident or a nurse. Strangely enough, that made me feel better, because as long as the baby was healthy and the birth normal, I knew I would be calm.

The day before I went into labor, I could still touch my toes. I started feeling contractions on the Sunday of my thirty-ninth week, but I didn't think much of them because they felt like the Braxton-Hicks I had felt for the past three months. Then, at 12:30 a.m. on Monday I began to feel an increase in the intensity of each contraction. I used my yoga breathing to get through them. My cervical plug had already come out, and I decided it was time to notify the doctor. He told me to come to the hospital. The nurse's examination showed I was already six centimeters dilated! No one could believe it.

If I had to rate the pain, I would say it was four out of a high of ten. The doctor broke my water (an unnecessary intervention, I found out later). After two more contractions, I was fully dilated. Three contractions later my daughter, weighing 5 pounds, 14 ounces, was born.

My labor and delivery went so fast that even the doctor was astounded.

I hadn't needed any medication. I was in such good shape that I was back in my old clothes in three weeks, with the health and energy I needed for my beautiful, active and healthy daughter.

G-d was watching me, making sure that I wound up in that internship despite my frustration, so that I could learn yoga, which turned out to be a wonderful exercise for me.

FYI...

Yoga is a wonderful exercise for pregnant women as well as for women with fertility problems, for several reasons: 1) It gets you into good physical shape and brings your weight to the most healthful point for you. (Even being underweight can create fertility problems.) 2) It relieves stress. 3) It makes the entire body work more efficiently so that the ligaments and muscles will be flexed and prepared. 4) Some of the postures target the reproductive organs, helping them work better.

Yoga and aerobics also help a woman have a healthier pregnancy and more stamina for the birth.

The American College of Obstetrics and Gynecologists (ACOG) recommends:

In the absence of medical or obstetrical complications, thirty minutes or more of moderate exercise a day, on most if not all days of the week, is recommended for pregnant women.

The Canadian Guidelines go one step further and say that physicians should be aware of the potential risks of their patients *not* exercising during pregnancy. See the following studies: J. C. Dempsey, C. L. Butler, and M.A. Williams, "No Need for a Pregnant Pause: Physical Activity May Reduce the Occurrence of Gestational Diabetes Mellitus and Preeclampsia, *Exercise and Sport Sciences Reviews*, vol. 33, no.. 3, pp. 141–149, and T. L. Weissberger, "The Role of Regular Physical Activity in Preeclampsia Prevention," in *Medical Science Sports Exercise,* vol. 36, no. 12 (December 2004), pp. 2024–31.

Before beginning any exercise program, it is wise to check with your caregiver. Low-impact aerobics and pregnancy yoga are ideal. It is important to take a class with a certified instructor who will advise you if it isn't too late to begin, what exercises could be too strenuous, and remind you to take in enough fluids and other precautionary measures. But give yourself and your baby a great gift — exercise.

A note to husbands: Please make sure your wife has the time to exercise without feeling pressured or guilty.

On Childbirth and the Redemption

Tamar Ansh

My sister had her third baby a few weeks ago. When she had her first, a boy, she asked me to accompany her. When she had her second, it happened on Shabbos and so fast that I didn't make it there in time. This time, she decided that I didn't need to come. She felt she would be okay, and wanted to relieve me of the unknown hours potentially spent in the delivery room and wondering how I would organize my childcare.

One morning, at 5:45 a.m., my phone started to ring incessantly. Too tired to hear it, I slept on until my cell phone started ringing.

"Hello," I managed to mutter.

"I'm in the hospital." It was my sister. "Complications. I know I said I didn't need you, but can you come?"

I heard the unspoken urgency in her voice. "Are you sure?" I knew that she had decided to hire a doula.

"Yes," she answered, unequivocally relieved. "And bring lots of food!"

With the adrenaline pulsing through my veins, I dressed quickly in comfortable clothes, sent the children off to school earlier than usual, organized who would take them all the rest of the day, and, with an army's worth of food and drink, set off for the hospital.

What had begun as a few minor complications soon turned into a "we must have this baby today and we will be inducing you now" kind of birth. My sister started off chipper and happy. Her husband was a good source of support, she was excited to have her baby, and besides, I had arrived with all the food. Soon, though, the pace of the labor increased. After several hours, the labor coach and I were not just relaxing and talking with her, but coaching and helping in earnest.

Every so often, a midwife would come in to check on her and see where we were holding, up the Pitocin level in the IV drip, and disappear. When she was checked at 3:30 p.m., they told her she was progressing nicely, but was still at the beginning stages. Things stepped up a bit more. Now the going was really getting rough. She was very uncomfortable, although tolerating it remarkably quietly. I envied her the naturalness of it all, the dignity of being able to handle it so well.

It was now 4:35 p.m., one hour since the last time she had been checked. She was in a lot of pain. I called for the midwife again, hoping to hear that we were almost at the end. The day had gone by very quickly and I had an additional pressure upon me now — it was close to suppertime, my friend who had my kids needed me to come back for them, and the kids themselves were worn down and upset that Mommy hadn't been home all day long. "Order pizza," I told my friend. "What was pizza invented for if not times like this!"

I suddenly remembered that there is a known

segulah to wear a ruby when in labor; it is supposed to speed up labor and help smooth the birth. I was wearing a ruby ring that day. Amazing. I took it off my hand and put it on hers.*

I was feeling pulled in two directions. On the one hand, I had not committed myself to staying beyond suppertime, as my sister's husband and labor coach were both there, and she herself had told me that she did not really need me. Of course, I wanted to stay for the birth once I had been there all day, but my obligations to my children pressed on me. On the other hand, my sister was now really in the thick of it and she pleaded with me not to go. "Ask her to take the kids a bit longer — I need you here." How could I leave my sister in such a state?

The midwife finally came in to check her. We were all hoping, since she was in such deep labor, that she was almost done. We were terribly dismayed to hear, though, that it was just the opposite. She was barely halfway there.

It took all my energy not to weep openly at that piece of news. We had all been working so hard. Not even halfway there and already in the kind of pain that only comes at the end? The labor coach and I tried to console her and keep our dismal thoughts from showing.

It was now 4:50 p.m. I absolutely *had* to be home before 6:30, no matter what.

In between breaths, my sister asked me what she could take. We started talking about taking some laughing gas to tide her over a bit longer.

Several more intense minutes crept by. The childbirth pains increased. Then my sister told the labor

---

* A ruby is said to strengthen the uterus and is worn to prevent miscarriage. Some rabbis say to remove it at the onset of labor, while others say to leave it on until after the birth.

coach that the baby was coming!

Impossible! I thought to myself. *Just barely ten minutes ago she was not even halfway there!*

When she repeated herself, the labor coach and I looked at each other. "It can happen, you know," she said to me. I called the midwife again, hoping to get someone who would be a bit friendlier and not give us trouble about checking her again so fast.

"She's right!" the midwife exclaimed. "The baby is right here."

One more minute, a little more coaching, and the baby was born. Right there in front of my eyes! We were all so stunned, and my sister was so worn out, that it took a few seconds to register what had happened.

The baby started to howl and I collected my wits and cried out to my brother-in-law, standing behind the curtain, "Do you hear? It's born! It's a boy!"

It was now 5:15 p.m., exactly the right time for me, too. I could now make it home, guilt free, on time for my children.

We all cried. We called my parents overseas to let them know the good news, stood around and marveled for a few more minutes, and then said a hasty goodbye as I ran out to my car.

I simply couldn't believe what I had just witnessed.

The whole way home, and the whole rest of the night, I was overcome with so many thoughts, so many turbulent emotions.

Klal Yisrael is hurting. Wherever you look there are difficulties, both on an individual and a national level. We all thought that the Holocaust would be the final labor pain before Mashiach, but here we are, more than sixty years later, and he is still not here…

Our Sages compare the coming of our Final Redemption to childbirth. I used to think that this comparison referred to those times when a woman was in labor and there was no relief: no laughing gas, no Demerol, no epidurals. Although women were in better shape — their daily lives being a real physical workout — some women suffered terribly.

Nowadays, we take it for granted that we will have a bit of a hard time during birth, but it will be okay. Yes, our Sages compare the Redemption to childbirth, but the experience could be closer to childbirth in our own times, with our various means of pain relief. So I thought to myself: *Let us pray, let us beseech the Master of the World — send us an epidural to get us through these labor pains. Please, help us that it should not hurt so badly while we are waiting for the birth!*

But that day a clear understanding hit me.

Our nation's birth pangs before Mashiach are high, hard, and coming too fast. We grasp at straws to keep ourselves afloat, but it seems like the end will never come, G-d forbid. The pains are so bad! And when the "midwife" comes to check on us, it seems that we are not even halfway there — *gevald*! Our Rabbis keep telling us that we need to have faith, to hang on, to believe. It is so hard to hear what they are saying. But look: right here, G-d threw the answer in my face.

Many experienced with birth know that when the woman says that she "can't take it anymore," it is a sure sign that the baby is coming. It is also known that the Talmud says, "The Redemption will not come until *klal Yisrael* despairs of it coming" (*Sanhedrin* 97a). How so?

There are several answers to this question, but if the Redemption is compared to childbirth, then the answer should be obvious! True, we may anesthetize ourselves and escape the pain with modern-day pain relievers:

fancy cars, homes, clothes, vacations. But childbirth involves a loss of control. When we release ourselves, when we let go and cry to Hashem that we "can't take it anymore"…that is when the Redemption will arrive! It is not the time for an epidural. It is the time for the delivery!

And who knows? Maybe then we will also be able to "finish in time to get home to our children" and finally see the fulfillment of the verse in the Prophets that says: "And return the hearts of fathers to their sons and the hearts of sons to their fathers" (*Malachi* 3:24).

> Tamar Ansh is the author of four books to date, as well as a food article writer. Her works include: *Splitting the Sea*, a collection of inspiring stories on *shidduchim*, (Targum Press); *A Taste of Tradition*, a gluten-free and non-*gebrochs* Pesach cookbook (Feldheim Publishers); *A Taste of Challah – and many other breads, too!* a complete guide to the art of challah making as well as many other tasty and healthy breads (Feldheim Publishers); and *Let's Say Amen!*, an illustrated children's book on the importance of Amen, (Feldheim Publishers).

FYI…

A Pitocin induction can be very painful. This is because the body's natural oxytocin is not released right away and therefore endorphins, the human's pain relief system, do not balance the pain of the induction. Raising the Pitocin level every twenty minutes can cause serious contractions, increasing the pain beyond what is manageable. It is worth asking if the Pitocin can be raised slowly. This can reduce fetal distress, reduce the need for an epidural, and reduce the risk of a cesarean.

A recent study also shows that induction doubles a woman's risk for an amniotic-fluid embolism, a leading cause of maternal death (albeit rare). See M. Kramer, "Induced Labor Is Tied to Maternal Risk," *Lancet*, vol. 368, pp. 1444–1448 (October 21, 2006).

My Brother's Wedding

Penina Lerner

Ten years of waiting, ten frustrating years of looking for "Mrs. Right." One broken engagement and dozens of *shidduchim*. And now, three years after my wedding, he had found her. Malka was twelve years old when my big brother, Moshe, had started going out. I suppose she was still jumping rope; he just had to wait.

Now, with the volcanic day a short two months away, the plans were being made quickly. The joy and excitement in our family, and in theirs, knew no bounds, especially since Malka's sister had married Moshe's best friend.

And I was anticipating the birth of my second child, due to make an appearance the same week. With a *tefillah* in my mouth from morning till night, I pleaded with Hashem to make sure I was at Moshe's *chuppah*.

I was crazy about Moshe's wife-to-be, so I was thrilled to help her plan this wedding. As the big day approached, my pounding heart and whirling thoughts kept me from sleeping as the "to do" list on my nightstand kept growing. The nervousness and excitement I had felt before my own wedding resurged during those two months.

Now, two days before my given due date, I was dressing in an aquamarine, maternity, sister-of-the bride gown. (It's incredible what you can buy or rent these days.) Looking regal and feeling so happy, I had made it to my brother's wedding day without a sign of labor — until now. As I closed the last snap on my gown, I felt it; that unmistakable pull of a contracting uterus.

No, no, no, Hashem, I thought. *I've been good for two months — davened, gave extra tzedakah, baked challah. All I asked for in return is to be at Moshe's chuppah.*

Ten minutes later, another tug. Maybe this wasn't labor. I straightened my *sheitel*, fixed my makeup, and there it was, another unmistakable cramp.

The photographer was on his way. We had to be at the hall in half an hour. We ordered a taxi. When we arrived in the hall, I let my mom in on my secret. However, I was there! I was at the hall! Solidifying family memories, the photographer called out, "Smile."

"One second," I said, pretending to adjust the band on my umpire-style dress. Actually, I was breathing through a contraction, the type one gets as things are getting a bit more real. For my sake, the sometimes tedious and drawn-out picture-snapping before the *chuppah* was rushed a bit.

As we moved through more of the protocol, I talked to Hashem once again. *I love my brother. We've waited for years. Please let me be at the chuppah.*

As the crowd began to assemble to escort Moshe to the *badeken*, I breathed slowly and deeply. Walking with the rest of the women down to the *chuppah*, I thought,

Please don't let my waters open, and then, *May they be blessed with a fulfilled life.*

The last blessing pronounced, I located my husband, softly screaming, "We have to go now!" We sped to the hospital, located just five minutes away. Changing from one gown to another, I pushed out our little son ten minutes after arriving. I had made Moshe's *chuppah*!

Waterfalls

Shabbos Surprise in Manchester

Bayla Devorah Topperman

I had just entered my seventh month of pregnancy and was enjoying the summer spell of weddings that were taking place. However, as the first in my class to get married and the first to be pregnant, I was feeling just a little sorry for myself, that I couldn't dance quite as much as all of my friends, and I found myself wishing out loud that the baby be born already! My family kept telling me to watch what I said — and I should have!

One morning, my husband and I were feeling quite tired and decided to sleep in a little. I had just under seven weeks to go until my estimated due date (the key word here is "estimated"). At 7:50 a.m. that Wednesday morning, the bag of water suddenly opened. At first I thought I must be mistaken, but with a puddle forming around me, I knew I was not! We quickly jumped out of bed, got dressed, put a few things into a bag, and set off for the hospital — in rush hour! Not knowing what to expect, as it was my first baby, all I could think about was having the baby in the car as we were stuck in traffic!

Baruch Hashem, we made it to the hospital. As I entered the labor ward, a kind Irish midwife asked me what had happened. I said, "I think my waters have broken."

She looked at my drenched clothes and the water trailing all down the corridor and said, "I think they have!"

Since I was only thirty-three weeks pregnant, they wanted to postpone labor for as long as possible and give me steroid injections to mature the baby's lungs. I was therefore put on the prelabor ward. Every evening at 8:00 p.m. and every morning at 4:30 a.m., I would start to get contractions, which would disappear after I took my medication!

Before Shabbos my husband and I decided that he should stay home and walk over to the hospital to see me on Shabbos afternoon. As the hospital was an hour-and-a-half walk from where we lived and involved walking through some rough areas, I advised him to walk with some friends.

I had been in the hospital for three days already with no signs of labor, so I thought that nothing would happen over Friday night and Shabbos morning. My husband said that he would be with me at about 2:30 on Shabbos afternoon.

On Shabbos morning, I again woke up with contractions at about 4:30. I was put on the monitor again and tried to go back to sleep. By 8:00, the contractions were still coming and I was moved to the labor ward. The contractions were quite irregular and short, and so I prepared myself for what I thought would be a long haul. I decided to daven and keep myself mobile, while using the Swiss antenatal breathing techniques during contractions.

By noon, the contractions were becoming very intense, so I asked the doctors if they could let me know what was happening. They hadn't been doing regular internal exams for fear of introducing germs and bacteria.

Lo and behold, I was five centimeters opened! "Do you want us to ring your husband in the prearranged manner?" the nurse asked.

Thinking that I still had a while to go, and that my husband said that he would be here by 2:30, I responded, "No, he'll be here this afternoon. I'm sure that he'll make it in time."

Well, he didn't! After the examination, labor progressed very quickly, and my beautiful daughter was born at 2:51 p.m., weighing 3 pounds, 8 ounces. She was immediately taken to the neonatal unit. My husband arrived at 4:30 p.m. with four of his friends. As the nurses from the prelabor ward hadn't told him what had happened, he walked into my labor room, asking me why I was on the labor ward. Imagine his surprise when I said, "*Mazal tov*, Tatte! We've got a baby girl!"

All he could say was, "But you look no different than when I left you yesterday before Shabbos. What do you mean you've had the baby?" The hospital staff was quite amused.

My Chava Yaffa had to spend just over two weeks in the neonatal unit until we were allowed to go home — a very short time considering that she was six weeks early and so small. I expressed my milk while Chavale was fed through a nasogastric tube, and she became strong and healthy in no time. Next time, though, I'll be watching what I say!

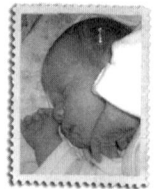

Surprisingly Simple

Rivka Elisheva (Barbara) Bennett

After having gone through an intense labor, with two-and-a-half hours of painful pushing, lots of stitches, and quite a recovery after the blessed birth of our first child, I didn't know quite what to expect just eighteen months later with the impending arrival of our second.

To make matters even more complicated, I was already past my due date — which wasn't particularly ideal, especially with Pesach right around the corner, falling on *motza'ei Shabbos*. Fortunately, we had recently moved to the very same neighborhood where my birthing coach, Sara, lived, so I was relieved to know that she was just a couple blocks away. However, the not-so-good news was that her one "blackout" date during the year was seder night, as that was a time reserved for her family, understandably so.

Much to everyone's relief, particularly my dear husband, we made it through Shabbos and *yom tov* and it wasn't until the tail end, literally, as the sun was setting, that I began to have contractions. Although they were mild, they were quite close together, so we diligently phoned Sara right after Havdalah. She advised that I pack my bag, take a shower, have a bite to eat, and be ready to go within an hour. Even though that didn't seem like a lot of time, somehow she seemed to have a premonition that this wasn't going to be a long, drawn-out affair.

The one wrinkle we did run into was that all the arrangements we had made for our one-and-a-half-year-old somehow fell through, so we had to scramble to come up with an alternative. *Baruch Hashem,* a relatively newly married couple we knew was only too happy to change their plans and come to stay with Esti.

The contractions began to get closer, but they were still mild, so I wasn't too worried, but when Sara arrived at the house as I was getting out of the shower, she encouraged us not to dillydally.

I sat down to enjoy some *matzah brei* my hubby had just cooked up. Then our friends strolled in. We were so busy chatting away that we didn't seem to hear Sara recommending that we call a cab and be on our way.

My husband finally got around to calling, and, just as he hung up the phone, I experienced what felt like a water balloon popping between my legs where I stood on the kitchen floor.

"Oh, no, I think my water just broke!" I exclaimed.

At that point, Sara took charge, instructing my husband to grab a towel and politely demanding that we leave the house immediately.

Once inside the cab, Sara urged me to fight against the contractions and began wondering out loud whether we should change our plans and go to a different hospital, which was five minutes closer.

I truly couldn't understand why she was so nervous, because even though I was certainly feeling uncomfortable, the labor, thus far, had been quite easy, and it wasn't as if I felt like pushing.

We safely marathoned into the maternity ward and Sara calmly, but quickly, related my status to the midwife in the reception office.

After briefly examining me, I was quite shocked when the midwife announced, "Okay, your baby is right here. Can you make it across the hall to the delivery room or would you like me to deliver you right here?"

Wow, that's great, I thought. *I'm fully dilated and it all happened so quickly and without much pain.*

Since I had just ambled into the reception office, I figured it wouldn't be a big deal to walk across the hall, so off we went.

They strapped a fetal monitor on me and it was already time to start pushing. After a couple of rounds, I soon realized that the contractions were only painful when I pushed, so I sheepishly admitted to Sara that I didn't want to push. She responded by telling me not to be afraid of the contractions and to follow my body's lead.

Before I knew it, a mere ten minutes later, I had the G-d-given privilege of pushing a beautiful baby girl into the world. My husband barely managed to finish registering me, making it into the delivery room just in time for the big moment and to have the opportunity to hold his brand-new baby girl.

After the long and painful overnight ordeal which had surrounded the birth of our first daughter, my husband was just thrilled with the "efficiency" of this one.

"Way to go, Mommy!" he exclaimed. "Wow, I can actually get some sleep tonight."

Once the excitement had died down, the baby was

taken to the nursery, my husband and Sara went on their way, and I was left alone with my thoughts. I simply couldn't get over the fact that everything had gone so quickly and smoothly, that Hashem had blessed us with a healthy child and that, somehow, for some reason, I had merited having such an easy birth this time around.

The next morning, Chol HaMo'ed, my husband was called to the Torah for the naming of our daughter. We joyously gave her the name Sara, after Sara Imeinu, and my dear grandmother, who had passed away within the year.

When my husband had the opportunity to look at the Torah reading during which he had received his aliyah, he was overwhelmed to discover that it was the very *pesukim* in *Parashas Emor* that instruct the Jewish people, over and over again, not to transgress Shabbos or *yom tov* — most appropriate to our precious *neshamah*, who was so sensitive to the *kedushah* of Shabbos and *yom tov* that she waited until *motza'ei yom tov* to make her debut...practically slipping out all by herself!

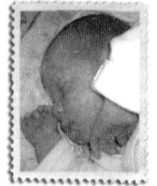

Nesting

Naomi Freeman

It was week 34 of a perfectly normal pregnancy when I woke up with an intensely strong burst of nesting syndrome. A bright sunny day beckoned me to take my toddler out to romp in the nearest park, but I chose instead to stay inside rearranging drawers and shelves. My goal was to clear out space for the soon-to-be needed, still-packed-away, infant outfits and necessities.

Our home was a third-floor, one-bedroom apartment where space was of such a high premium that only careful arrangement and orderliness would make it comfortable for the soon-to-be four of us in those small, cramped quarters. Tamar, our two-year-old, watched me in wonder as the day progressed and I endlessly sorted and sifted through one drawer and closet after another. She kept up an ongoing chatter with me about all kinds of subjects and we were enjoying our time together when finally, after hours of hard work, I reached the finale. Now all I needed to do was climb up on the kitchen stool to reach the highest upper cabinet and pull out the box of infant-size cloth diapers to be relocated into the top drawer of the changing table in our bedroom.

Given that I was quite physically active throughout my pregnancy, walking briskly every day, I thought nothing of ascending onto the stool and stretching up to reach the goal of my whole nesting day. But as I was standing up high, I suddenly lost my balance, slipping and toppling right onto my distraught daughter! Tamar started to wail and I immediately wrapped my arms around her and tried to comfort her. "Oh, did I hurt you? What hurts you?" I said as soothingly as possible, though it was obvious that I had landed on her foot.

When we both calmed down a bit, I shakily stood up and only then noticed that the floor was wet. Had I knocked over a cup of water on my way down? Did Tamar, in her fright, have an accident?

The back of my dress felt damp, so I turned to examine it. I saw a perfectly round circle of wet on the blue material.

Uh-oh! In the impact of my fall, amniotic fluid had burst out of me! I lumbered quickly to the phone to call my midwife, Sharon, and tell her what happened. "Naomi," she practically shouted into the phone, "please go to the hospital right away!"

I definitely didn't want to do that. "Oh, no, Sharon, I don't want to go to the hospital! I need to get off my feet and stay in bed! If we go now, it could be hours before I'm able to lie down and rest! I don't want to walk around at all! It's much safer for me to stay at home!" I pleaded with her.

I called my husband at yeshivah to inform him of our dilemma. I tried to stay calm, while waiting for both him and Sharon to show up. When Sharon came, she immediately checked the baby and determined that the heartbeat was good and strong, but unfortunately, contractions had started up. I wished that I could go back and do the day over again without having attempted such a silly feat as climbing up on a stool! What had I been thinking?

The danger of PROM (Premature Rupture Of Membranes) is infection, but I was more worried about the germs lurking in the hospital than the ones that my body was already used to in our home. Our primary concern was preventing a six-week prematurely born baby! I was extremely anxious about being subjected to internal exams, inspections, and injections that could inadvertently introduce unwanted bacteria into my body.

I prayerfully pleaded with G-d to help my baby stay inside, where it was warm and safe. "You need to keep growing and developing until your real due date!" I said silently to my unborn child. "Please stay inside six more weeks!"

Since I so adamantly refused to go to the hospital, Sharon reluctantly agreed to let me stay at home, with the following conditions: contractions had to stop within a few hours, and I had to drink copious amounts of fluids to replace what I'd lost. In addition, I was to ingest Vitamin C and an anti-infection herbal tincture of echinacea and propolis. Monitoring my temperature was a must, and if there was any hint of fever, we had to leave promptly. Lying in bed, visualizing my womb, I imagined a resilient bubble already patched, the accidental breach in my amnimotic sac healing up into a strong, viable whole once again.

In less than twelve hours, the slow drizzle of amniotic fluid ceased to flow and the irregular contractions had stopped completely. There was no hint of fever. In contact by phone, Sharon insisted that I stay in bed for the next five days straight, keeping pressure off the pelvic floor. After that, no heavy work or lifting. No hauling heavy groceries up the three flights of stairs to our apartment. Over the next few weeks, she continued to come to monitor me and the baby. Everything, *baruch Hashem*, was fine.

My daughter enjoyed having a "captive" Imma all to herself, as we read stories together and she played with toys on the edge of my bed. The babysitter took her to the park in the afternoon and my husband took care of the laundry, meals, and everything else. Though it was challenging staying in bed so long (and boring too), I figured an enforced rest wasn't so bad for a usually overactive mother.

Thankfully, we eventually made it to the fortieth week. Exactly on my estimated due date, a normal labor began. Seven hours later, with great relief and gratitude to G-d, we greeted our biggest baby ever — an 8.5 pound boy!

The moral of the story? Be careful to avoid heavy-duty cleaning, no matter how much you enjoy it! It can really be risky for you and your baby!

> P.S. After our son was born, the midwife, upon examining the placenta, discovered a rare condition called "velamentous insertion," where the cord is attached to the placenta, running along the membranes rather than directly into the placenta. Miraculously, my waters, which had completely sealed up after that initial premature rupture, remained intact until the exact moment my son was born. AROM, Artificial Rupture of Membranes, done routinely in many hospitals, could have caused his death, G-d forbid, if the rupture had inadvertently detached his cord.

FYI...

There's an expression in *The Thinking Woman's Guide to a Better Birth* by Henci Goer: "If it ain't broke, don't break it." The amniotic fluid is a temperature regulator and allows the fetus to move more easily, buffering it against intense contractions. In G-d's goodness, He created the perfect environment for a baby to grow and be protected. Every second is precious for the fetus.

Who are we to end the birth before its time? There are rare situations when a baby is crowning still with the sac intact. Then the caregiver really needs to open up the sac.

I once had a woman interview me for the upcoming birth of her fourth child. As we spoke, she mentioned that her water never breaks on its own. The doctor always does it for her. "How open are you when that happens?" I asked her. "About five or six centimeters," she answered.

Occasionally, a woman will stall at six, seven, or eight centimeters, and opening the sac will help the baby descend, putting pressure on the cervix to dilate more. However, the ideal solution is position changes and old-fashioned, low-tech patience.

Emotions and past childbirth issues can also stop labor from progressing. This is a time to "let go and let G-d."

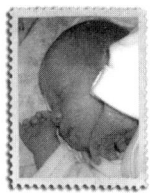

The Postponed Barbeque

Libby

Married less than five months, we discovered that our soon-to-be addition to the family was going to be two additions! The pregnancy continued uneventfully, and we kept our secret from everyone except our parents.

Although August was three months away, we had already booked our doctor and a doula (labor assistant). I was taking childbirth education classes during which I was told twins could be born early. (I thought it wise to inform my childbirth educator of my situation.)

One sunny Thursday morning in my thirty-first week, I woke up feeling a bit wet. When I mentioned this to my husband, he responded, "Well, it can't be your waters because you'll know it when it breaks. Must be part of the pregnancy."

Okay, I thought. *I'll finish making Shabbos and then we'll go to our evening barbeque and watch the sunset over the ocean in Netanyah.*

After packing up the car and heading out of Jerusalem, I had a gut feeling to call my doula. She said, "It may not be anything, but it's worth checking it out at the hospital." A bit upset by the delay of a barbecue, to the hospital we went.

"One hundred percent effaced and three centimeters dilated with amniotic fluid leaking," was not exactly what we wanted to hear. It seemed like it was a "high leak," but it was amniotic fluid nonetheless. I was immediately put on steroids to strengthen the babies' lungs and magnesium to prolong the labor. Contractions were coming every five minutes, but I barely felt them.

My calm and cautious doctor arrived, informing us that if the labor progressed and I delivered within twenty-four hours, it would be by cesarean. He didn't want to take any chances, and knowing that the second baby was in a breech position made for another minor setback. Of course we wanted healthy babies, first and foremost, but I'd had my heart set on a natural birth. After a cesarean, I would be considered high-risk during subsequent births, and we wanted to avoid that.

When we called my parents, they asked, "Did you get a second opinion? Did you speak to another doctor?" It hadn't even occurred to us before, and we immediately picked up the phone to call my wide-thinking childbirth educator. She began calling other doctors who would possibly take on this case, asking them my chances of a regular birth. "A second twin who is breech has a good chance of turning head down once the first one is born," she said. "However, the fact that they are so small..."

By now it was 10:45 p.m., and people weren't interested in getting involved. One doctor didn't want to

The Postponed Barbeque

take a case away from a colleague. Finally, one doctor said we should call him in the morning.

In the meantime, the medication stalled the contractions to about fifteen to twenty minutes apart, and the staff told us that there was a possibility of the medication stalling the birth for up to three weeks, although there were no guarantees.

After a restless sleep due to the unknowns, I woke with weak contractions coming every forty-five minutes. The "new" doctor came to examine me and look at my file before making the decision whether to take on my case. Anxiety rose as we waited for his "verdict." *Court cases must be like this before the gavel pounds down*, I thought. At last, he gave a "heads up" regarding the possibility of a natural birth, and being that he had delivered hundreds of breech babies, he wasn't concerned about that either, especially since it was the second twin that was breech.

The only hurdle to overcome was the transfer to the hospital where he practiced, which was an hour and a half away. I asked my doula to assist in calling an ambulance for the hospital-to-hospital transfer while I rested and my husband packed the bags.

"No way am I taking her," said the first driver. "Not unless there's a doctor or midwife coming with us."

"One and a half hours away? We aren't willing to do it," said the next.

"Twins? So who's coming with us?" said the third.

And on and on it went, until she called ambulance number eight, giving him minimal information so he would agree to the transfer.

By now the contractions were really light, once an hour. We waited for the ambulance to show up.

"Forget it!" was the driver's first reaction when he

heard the nurse's scream he shouldn't do it and the danger was too great. He wanted money for having come for nothing and off he drove.

Left in a stupor, feeling trapped and ready to cry, I called our new doctor (Dr. X). By now the original doctor had been told of our decision to switch doctors, and he was less than thrilled at our "irresponsible" decision. Dr. X said I could go in a Mercedes or other smooth-riding car and I would be fine. At still three centimeters (having been checked that morning), I felt confident we could make it, but not confident enough to go alone.

I called my doula, asking her if she knew of a taxi driver with a comfortable Mercedes. She arranged the driver, and agreed to accompany us. So, early Friday afternoon, she said good bye to her family, saying, "See you before Shabbos, G-d willing."

The smooth, calming ride in the tan, leather-upholstered, air-conditioned car was just what I needed after the harrowing uncertainty of the past eighteen hours.

After we arrived at the new hospital, I sent my doula back to Jerusalem, wishing her a good Shabbos.

"Oh, no!" Two hours later, my contractions began again and were now just a few minutes apart. The midwife who examined me pronounced me at four centimeters, adding, " Your doctor and doula may not make it in time." Just the comforting thoughts I needed to hear at that point.

Just as we ushered in Shabbos, my doctor and my doula arrived. My doula assisted in easing my back labor pains. However, when the labor seemed to stall at seven centimeters at 10:30 p.m., I opted for an epidural. The pain became more manageable, but was far from disappearing. My husband and doctor sang *zemiros* and made Kiddush, which let me, for a brief moment, think about the merit of giving birth in the land of Israel with an observant doctor and surrounded by Jewish staff.

After an hour with no progress, my doula said suddenly, "What nice stones you're wearing around your neck. Where did you get them?"

"From Devorah Feister," was my reply.

"What?" She was stunned. "Let's take those off immediately," she said more calmly as she helped me remove them.

Devorah was a woman who knew a lot about stones, and she had given them to me to prevent miscarrying. Although I do not understand the power of stones, the Talmud does talk about them for healing and other uses.

As the contractions finally continued, strong and steady, my first daughter was born, without a cut or tear, at 12:05 a.m. A few minutes later and with one push, my second daughter was born in breech position. I had let the epidural wear off, so I could feel the intensity of the contractions. What a thrill to birth my babies. I felt a rush of adrenalin as they showed me our daughters, so frail looking but with the strong cries of full-term babies, I was told. The support in the intensive care was more than we could have asked for. I managed to pump and give them my milk until after we arrived home, at which point I alternated between bottle- and breastfeeding.

We came home three weeks before their intended birthday.

Over those few weeks, we had witnessed many calming, orange sunsets while the girls were gaining strength. And just before heading home, we finally had our barbeque.

Birth from Above

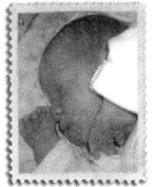

The Right Way Up

Nechama Krinsky

They must have thought I was drunk on the bus, grinning away and even giggling from time to time. I was returning from a routine ultrasound that was to determine my due date. Not understanding what I was seeing, I watched the screen with interest, eager to get a glimpse of what was to be my seventh baby. After moving around the transducer for what seemed like an unusually long time, the technician asked, "Why did your doctor send you for an ultrasound?" Something about her voice put me on alert.

"He wants to know how far along I am. Is everything okay?" I asked in trepidation.

"Yes, yes," she reassured me. "I have a surprise for you."

What could it be? For a flash I thought, *Maybe twins.* Oh yeah, right.

"You're having twins," she said.

I always thought twins went to organized people. I giggled so much the technician had trouble keeping the transducer in place.

After I was handed my papers, I exited from the wrong door, into the storeroom. On the way to the bus stop I bumped into two or three strangers, finally finding my way on to the bus and into a seat. All the way home, I amused myself with thoughts of how my husband would receive the joyous tidings.

"Got a picture?" he asked as I walked in.

"Yes. I'll show you after we put the kids to bed."

At nine-thirty that evening, my husband returned from his late-night meeting and sat down to hear about my day. When I got to the technician's "I have a surprise for you," he said jokingly, "Twins." I nodded. "Nah," he said in his I'm-not-falling-for-that-one voice.

"Yes. Twins," I said, handing him the pictures.

"No," he said in disbelief, sitting down, stunned. "Two highchairs...two cribs...two everything!"

That night, I was still awake at three in the morning. Thoughts flooded my mind. What would I do if they both cried at night? I pictured myself trying to pick them both up at the same time. Would I be able to nurse? If yes, then both? At the same time?

By the seventh month, I still hadn't told my mother the double news, but it arrived to England accidentally through my Canadian cousin, who let it slip. I shouldn't have told him, but I didn't think it would cross continents.

Being a doctor as well as a mother, Mom immediately began to worry. "Get a good private gynecologist," were her orders.

At the first checkup, in my eighth month, we did an ultrasound and discovered twin breeches; both of them were head up!

"Let's see what position they're in during your next visit," was the doctor's reaction.

The Right Way Up

Due to my history of rather early births, I was instructed not to pick up any heavy objects and to avoid housework. Now that I didn't mind!

I had a friend who had carried double-breech babies. She received a special blessing from a Rebbe, and the babies turned while she was in labor, enabling her to have a natural delivery. I decided to call the Rebbe as well.

The Rebbe gave me a beautiful blessing in Hebrew, in which I heard the words *"raglayim lematah"* (legs down) loud and clear. "Oh, no," I wanted to say, "you've got it wrong — it's legs up and head down!" But I couldn't show such disrespect to the Rebbe. I thanked him for his blessing and then prayed that things would come out for the best.

Well, my husband had to go to the States for ten days. He was due to return five weeks before my estimated due date. We decided he should take along my two youngest, leaving me with no one to look after under the age of five.

"But what if I go into labor before you get back?"

"Don't worry," he answered with his usual optimism, "you won't."

On the Thursday night he was supposed to return, he called from New York. "The connecting flight was delayed and I missed the flight." Not only that, but "the next one won't arrive before Shabbos, so I'll have to leave on Sunday."

I never prayed so hard before.

My husband arrived home on Monday morning, just in time for that week's ultrasound. "Still face to face," the doctor said.

"Might they still turn around?" I asked hopefully.

"There's a possibility, but only slight," answered my doctor.

She decided to check me, only to find that I was four centimeters dilated. "I'd better monitor you. Are you feeling contractions?"

"No," I replied.

The monitor showed nice contractions, not the Braxton-Hicks I thought I was having.

"It looks like you're having strong ones. Let's admit you and see what the next few hours bring."

I called my husband, who called our doula to pick up my bags from home and meet me at the hospital. She arrived soon after. Within a couple of hours, I was six centimeters dilated with no change in the babies' positions.

The doctor offered to wait a little longer or to perform a cesarean immediately. Feeling impatient by now, I gave the go-ahead. It seemed fairly obvious that this was what G-d wanted.

My two healthy baby girls, weighing 5 pounds, 3 ounces, and 4 pounds, 3 ounces, were born one hour later.

I had to wait until the morning to nurse them, as they both were taken for observation. In the morning, Twin A (as the bracelet said) was bigger, round-faced, and very sleepy. Twin B seemed to get very little at the feed.

I was struggling to feed them for three days with no encouragement from the nurses, who kept suggesting I give them a bottle after only a few minutes of trying to nurse. My milk finally came in after the third day. I found out later that it takes a bit longer for the milk to come in after a cesarean, and it would have been okay to give a supplement until the nursing was well established in a few days' time. It was important to maintain the babies' weight.

Although Twin B had gained some weight by the

time I was ready to leave the hospital, she still wasn't up to five pounds on the sixth day. So, although I could go home, Twin B had to stay in the hospital. I had expressed enough milk for my husband to bring the bottles to the baby. When he arrived that evening with refills, they informed him that she now weighed two kilos and could go home.

In retrospect, even though a cesarean wouldn't have been my first choice, it did give me the chance to stay in the hospital for a few extra days. That gave me the opportunity to establish good nursing habits for both twins before arriving home. When I did arrive home, I had more emotional energy for the other children. I also had an unusually quick recovery. This was a marvelous lesson to me in trusting a Rebbe's blessing.

Right Decision, Wrong Reason

Yedida Silverstone

"Oh, what a terrible experience I had at hospital X. Now I only go to hospital Y. Isn't that where you go?"

"I hire a doula every time and it's wonderful. We labor at home for a good few hours and then..."

When I sit with other women as they discuss their many birth experiences, I tend to feel left out. I had only one birth experience — and that was a cesarean. But it has furnished me with a lot to tell.

One Sunday morning, in the middle of my ninth month, the ring of the telephone woke me up. As I bent over to reach for the receiver, something happened in my upper back. There was pain, but it was something more than that, though I couldn't say exactly what. Sunday passed with me staying in the recliner and getting up as little as possible. I was used to that part — it had been a high-risk pregnancy due to a chronic condition. I was being monitored constantly for high blood

Right Decision, Wrong Reason

pressure and low platelets, and I had been told to rest as much as possible.

But that day my bed was not comfortable, and getting up from it produced extreme pain — in fact, I could hardly straighten myself out. So my husband took off the Sealy mattress and replaced it with a firm foam rubber one. Someone suggested that perhaps the pain was early labor. We went to bed uneasily.

At 4:30 a.m. I awoke with suspicions that my waters had broken. They came out in a whoosh when I pulled myself up. Into a taxi — and off to the hospital!

At the hospital, where I was already well known, the doctors got together to decide whether I should be allowed to have a natural birth or not. A cesarean had been a probability from the beginning, though I had hoped that I would be allowed to experience a normal birth. In fact, at my last ultrasound I had asked whether the baby was a girl or a boy — I didn't want to be the last one to know…

Sometime around ten, they finally decided upon a cesarean after all, under full anesthesia. The reason for this decision was that women with low platelets can bleed more, so even during regular births they must avoid an epidural. Their fear was that the baby also had low platelets, in which case a regular birth, with all the pressures involved, might be dangerous.

I started to think about the surgery. I had had an operation as a child, but then I didn't know enough to be afraid. My chief fear was of being unconscious and not being able to pray if anything went wrong.

From that point on until the anesthesia took effect, I recited the verse, "*B'yadcha afkid ruchi, padisa osi Hashem Keil emes* — I put my life in Your hands, You redeemed me, Hashem, truthful G-d" (*Tehillim* 31:6), over and over again.

"Please, be careful when you switch me from bed to bed," I told the nurses. "I have a back problem." At 1:00 p.m. I was in the operating room, waiting. All at once the doctors swarmed in: "Okay, let's get going on this one."

I wasn't surprised by their speed. My sister-in-law had warned me that cesareans are performed very quickly so that the baby won't be affected by the anesthetic. In her case it had seemed like they were ready to make the cut before she had been anesthetized.

The mask was put over my mouth and nose, and I was told to count back from a hundred. The last thing I saw was the clock on the wall: 1:10, it read.

An instant later, or so it seemed, I was waking up. It was hard to believe it was all over, and that several hours had passed (unlike when one is asleep, under anesthesia there is absolutely no sense of time passing).

"You have a daughter," I was told.

"Is she okay?" was all I could croak.

"Yes," I was reassured.

My husband and in-laws were waiting for me outside. Up in the maternity ward, I was allowed to see the baby for a few minutes, and then they took her away — to monitor her for possible problems and to keep her warm. I couldn't hold her, anyway, due to the operation and the back pain. My baby was fine, with no platelet problem.

Six weeks later, the terrible back pain had not gone away. An X-ray of my back showed nothing unusual. "Your back muscles are just weak from the pregnancy," I was told. Physiotherapy didn't help me much, either. Finally, after another X-ray, the devastating diagnosis was made: severe osteoporosis. I had what are known as compression fractures in four vertebrae! No wonder I felt like my back was about to snap in half each time I moved.

The reason for this condition was simple: The cortisone I had been taking had leeched calcium out of my body. My doctors, for some inexplicable reason, had been very half-hearted in prescribing calcium supplements, even though I was unable to eat milk products or any other substantial source of calcium. I was not ingesting enough calcium, and whatever I did have went to the baby.

Thank G-d, there is treatment for osteoporosis, and a few weeks after the diagnosis I began to feel better, eventually being able to feed my daughter, dress her, and actually swoop her up from the floor (careful, there). I could even take her out for a walk in the especially light stroller we had bought.

But until that point, it was pure misery. Even holding a glass of water produced a twinge in my back. I was in pain, helpless, and terrified. The mental agony was, of course, far worse. I had just become a mother, but what kind of mother was I, not able to take care of her baby daughter? And would I ever recover?

But what carried me through — and still does — was the realization that had the doctors decided to allow me a regular birth, I probably wouldn't have been walking around at all. Imagine the result of all that pressure on a back that was like a pile of *cholent* chicken bones; imagine, also, what would have happened if they would have stuck an epidural needle among those crumbling vertebrae.

The doctors had made the right decision — for the wrong reason. They had thought that there might be a problem with the baby's platelets, and that was why they decided to perform a cesarean under full anesthesia. In the end, there was no platelet problem, but the cesarean probably saved my life. Yes, G-d was watching over me, and He made sure that a terrible mistake wasn't made.

People tend to get uptight when the possibility of a cesarean comes up. Of course, it's no fun (especially when it comes to recovering from it), and of course, it does carry more risk than a regular birth. But there are times when it is lifesaving to the mother, the baby, or both.

Then there's the matter of mother-baby bonding. I barely took care of my daughter for the first few months after birth, beyond giving orders to others to feed her and change her diaper, and looking over their shoulders as they did. I never held her comfortably when she was a baby. Our relationship, thank G-d, is far from being distant. For those of you who cannot care for your babies for one reason or another, don't make it harder for yourselves by getting uptight about possible long-term effects of this separation, painful as it might be.

I felt incapable of breastfeeding my daughter. My husband made a single attempt to convince me to do it anyway, but I insisted that I felt too weak. After the diagnosis was finally made, it became evident that my instincts had been one hundred percent right. Breastfeeding in my condition would have leeched even more calcium out of my body, and my baby wouldn't have gotten enough milk either. Of course, it's better to breastfeed, but if one can't, then one should be thankful for the existence of all those ready-made formulas. Isn't that what they're there for? Our little daughter thrived and is now a wonderful, active teenager, thank G-d.

Big Head Facing the Wrong Way

Sara Huberman

My first birth: twenty-three hours of labor, failure to progress, cesarean. It made me feel like a statistic. But this is not the story of my first birth. This is the story of my second birth. This time, I would be better prepared.

I was at nine months plus and I felt great. My two-year-old was finally sleeping through the night. My brisk, three-times a week walk made me feel great and look pretty rosy-cheeked for someone who was now officially past her due date. But, like all pregnancies, it couldn't last forever, and finally the day arrived. I had just been to my gynecologist that evening and the report was the same: nothing doing. I got to bed around midnight (not smart for a woman who could go into labor at any time), and, as usual, found myself awake at one to use the facilities.

I tossed and turned and couldn't fall back asleep. How frustrating! And there was my husband, rhythmically breathing in a deep sleep. I had my usual Braxton-

Hicks, stronger now, and I started to feel a little suspicious. I remembered this nervous, restless feeling at the beginning of labor from last time. I began to time my contractions and, lo and behold, although they were not yet strong, they were pretty consistent. Forgoing the fitful sleep, I got up and walked around.

I opened my *Tehillim* and talked to G-d, and now it was time to talk with my sister. In any case, she was "on call" for my sleeping beauty (who can you call in the middle of the night besides a single, college-age girl)? I called my mother in a different time zone and asked her to pray for me. I debated calling my labor coach. The debate was short-lived, and I reached for the portable phone as I drew the bath water.

Fourteen hours later, now in the hospital, we were in the midst of what felt like an electrical storm that is awesome to watch but scary to be within. I was now eight centimeters dilated and, as I sang my way through my contractions, I felt somewhat in control. But the baby was still high: minus 2 station. (This is considered engaged, but not at 0 station, which would have made me feel more relaxed.) Not to worry, there was still time… The doctor recommended that we break my waters. Okay. Was there any other option? I felt my strength waning. We were moving but too slowly, even for my liking.

Swoosh...! Suddenly I was standing in a puddle of green water. I was exhausted, and I was in more pain than I could ever have imagined.

We gave it a few more contractions. At last I was ten centimeters, but I was still at minus 2 station — not good. The posterior position of the baby was also not making things easier. When the baby is facing the front of the woman's body instead of towards her spine, a lot more room is needed to maneuver through the pelvis. If the baby's head is a large one, as mine was, the journey is even more challenging.

I don't know how I was still standing. I don't know how there could be so many people in this world, when they all had to be born this way, through the curse of Chavah. We tried to turn my body so the baby would turn. The baby flipped and flopped from side to side, but remained posterior.

All I wanted to do was sleep. But I couldn't. I wouldn't go calmly into the operating room, not until I had tried everything! Still, at minus 2 station, I realized that I was crying. I didn't mean to cry, but I was so drained and the baby wasn't coming down.

"Another forty-five minutes," the doctor said, "and then we'll try an epidural, which sometimes surprises us by relaxing the mother and bringing the baby down." Another forty-five minutes? I couldn't hold out that long. But I didn't say anything because I knew I had to try 100 percent. If I only went 99 percent, I would regret it later.

Although it feels like it, labor does not kill literally, only figuratively. I made it through another forty-five excruciating minutes of standing and moving and slipping in the green water. The monitor showed no fetal distress, which allowed me to lunge, hoola-hoop, and rock on my hands and knees. *Please G-d, please make this baby descend!* The doctor did another check. Still at minus 2 station. I cried, I shook, I gave up. Where was the anesthesiologist?

"We'll give you an hour with the epidural," I heard my doctor. "If nothing happens, then we have no choice." I knew it was still possible to have a regular birth, but I was more than resigned to the other possibility. I wasn't optimistic. I was a *shmatte* by then.

Where was the anesthesiologist already? He finally arrived. He looked familiar with his long, thick, jet-black ponytail. Why was he taking his time? He asked me to stop shaking. I couldn't. Somehow, I relaxed enough for him to give me the epidural. My labor coach tried to comfort me.

One hour later, I gave birth to a beautiful, healthy, 9-pound baby girl in the operating room. I knew that I had really won, but I also harbored a sense of loss. This time (as opposed to my first birth) I knew that I had covered all my bases, but G-d had decided otherwise. After the birth I had a strong wish to say a thanksgiving prayer to G-d that I was living in such a generation of modern technology, and that my baby and I were both alive and well.

And I also thank G-d for the gift of forgetfulness, because, G-d willing, when the time comes, I want to try again.

FYI...

When medically necessary, a cesarean can be a lifesaving technique and worth the risks. However, fifteen studies conducted in the past year show an associated increase of complications and mortality for mother and baby, so a cesarean should be done only when there are serious medical indications.

In 2004, 30.2 percent of all births were by cesarean section. Since 1996, the cesarean rate has climbed 46 percent. In fact, the cesarean rate has risen for the ninth year straight, according to preliminary birth data for 2005, recently released by CDC's National Center for Health Statistics (www.cdc.goc/nchs).

Women wrongly assume that a cesarean affects only *this* birth and *this* baby. In truth, cesarean births affect future pregnancies and births as well.

For an analysis of these findings, and for data concerning the risks of cesarean surgery and its effect on future pregnancies and births, visit the International Cesarean Awareness Network (ICAN) at www.icanonline.org/press/articles/20061121-ican.pdf.

A Second Chance

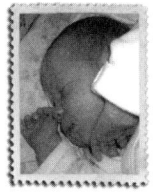

Blue Skies

Ellen Greenfield

"Blue skies, nothing but blue skies," my mind hums the old tune dreamily, as I lie for the first time on Dr. Frank's examining table. From my viewpoint, this is all I can see on this particular October morning.

As the doctor yanks the gray medical curtain around me, my view of the outside is suddenly obstructed. I am jolted back to the issue at hand. "Now let's have a look."

His manner is gentle and warm, without being intrusive. Later, as he leafs through my old medical records, I am sure he is shaking his head, closing the door on the possibility of a natural birth. He mumbles as he reads why I had a C-section the first time. "Ah," he sighs, "the baby was stuck in deep transverse arrest, unable to descend into a natural delivery." I can already hear the Wicked Witch of the West sneering, "Na na na na na — you're gonna have another C-section," as she flies wildly around my consciousness. I am in my fifth month, and this annoying apparition has been my ever-present companion ever since the birth of my daughter Meira by C-section three years before.

Shortly after making aliyah, David and I had shared a quiet moment in our Jerusalem garden. With G-d's help, I was expecting our second child. Yet I had been filled with anxiety, as thorny as the fragrant rosebushes that were surrounding us. Thinking about the pregnancy, the heavy door of childbirth creaks open. As one foot cautiously tries to get a toe through the crack, it is immediately squashed by witches and demons, vivid and painful memories of Meira's birth. David lovingly chided me, "Women have been giving birth for centuries. Besides, how do you know that this birth will be as bad as the last one?"

"You know what the score was last time. You know the way I felt right after the birth — it took me months to recover." Despite having a beautiful baby, I was haunted by feelings of failure. It had meant so much to me to have a natural birth. Now, who knew if I could even find a doctor willing to perform a VBAC (Vaginal Birth After Cesarean, pronounced "veeback")? The thought of having another "C," totally anesthetized, no pain, no participation, and no loving maternal presence for the newborn, made me sick. I hated the idea; I always had. And let's not forget my mother's mantra of how wonderful it was to be "out" when the baby (namely me) was born. Maybe this was okay for her in 1963, but it was not going to work for me in 1993.

David shrugged and flashed me a loving smile, and sighed as if to say, "There's nothing more I can say. This 'baby' is yours…" He got up from the table, taking the plate of half-eaten borekas with him, leaving me to clean the crumbs off the table and clear away the morsels of conflict in my heart.

And so, I began to look for a doctor who would be

willing to perform a VBAC. I found a beacon, someone who gave me a searchlight of hope. My yoga instructor, Rachel, raved about her obstetrician, Dr. Frank. "Look, Ellen," she said, reading the anxiety on my face, "he does VBACs. He's even willing to do a VBAC after two C's. This makes him sort of controversial. But don't worry about that, just go see him."

And see him I do. "I see no reason why you can't have a VBAC," Dr. Frank begins. "As a matter of fact, I don't see why Meira's birth couldn't have been natural."

"What?" I stammer. "What do you mean? How could that be?"

"It's simple," Dr. Frank continues. "I've delivered a lot of babies that were stuck in this position. It's not so uncommon. All it requires is some skillful manipulation to rotate the baby into a position where they can be delivered."

The Wicked Witch has been chased away by this pronouncement, and my consciousness is left fuming, as it vacilates between anger and exhilaration. I feel the door to natural delivery opening ever so slightly.

Despite medical assurance from my obstetrician, visions of another bad birth scene haunt me. Determined to fight them, I attend a birthing workshop in the middle of my sixth month. There I meet Tammy, a certified labor coach, who spoke about birth and spirituality in simple, loving terms that were comforting and reassuring. My last birth coach was so different. While she had meant well, her ideology and negative attitude towards medical intervention was a heavy load, weighing me down. Tammy was light, with a colorful scarf covering her hair, and she had a distinct aura of love and acceptance. I was drawn to her.

I asked her to be my labor coach; she smiled, cocked her head, and agreed. She asked me to come to her house to discuss a birth plan.

Upon entering her century-old home, I immediately felt connected to something holier and deeper. Like the strong, tall beams supporting her home, I felt myself relaxing, expanding, supported by Tammy's being. She sensed that there was something holding me back emotionally and invited me to do a guided visualization.

Comfortably ensconced on her fluffy white couch, I float into a trance-like state, as she hums a haunting and comforting tune. She is sitting cross-legged on the floor next to me, and whispers, "Now, Ellen, what do you need? What are you missing that you need to have this baby?"

"I don't know."

"It's okay, this takes some getting used to. Let yourself go to a place where you feel very safe, like a beach or garden. Now, what do you see?"

"I am walking in a garden," I respond in a detached voice. "There is a bridge at the end of the garden."

"And can you see anything at the end of the bridge?"

"Yes, it's my grandma."

Grandma was the typical loving, indulgent grandmother. She had passed on several years before.

Grandma could and would always be there for me. Her soft, Yiddish-accented voice brought me joy and comfort. Even now, tears come to my eyes at the memory of a little game she would play. Sitting in the old, green kitchen chair, she would stretch out her floury white arms, beckoning, "Come, come to me, *meidele*." I would do my best to leap into her lap, and melt into the warmth of Grandma's embrace.

Floating back to the visualization, Tammy gently encourages me to carry on. "Is your grandmother doing anything, saying anything?"

"No, but she's holding a present and she looks like she wants to give it to me."

"Then let her give it to you."

"Grandma..." She's close enough that I can feel the love emanating from her smile. But I am still in this world enough to know that this reunion is in my mind, in my soul, and that I can't really hug her, as much as I long to. "What have you brought me from the other world?"

She puts a small, beautifully wrapped square box into my shaking hands.

"It's for you, *mammale*, I want you should have it."

"But Grandma, what is it?" I persist.

"My darling, let's say it's a present of permission. I let you. I let you have this birth your way, not your mother's way. So she had C-sections, that's her *pekel*. Now you go on, I leave you my blessing to birth this child without the shackles of guilt." Her image fades away, and tears of sadness and joy envelope me. I open my eyes, and Tammy is smiling at me. As if to finish off the visualization, she hugs me and says, "Now I understand."

Early in my ninth month, I receive a call from Tammy.

"Ellen, I don't know if you heard."

"Heard what?" I brace myself.

"Dr. Frank lost the case. He will no longer be allowed to practice in the hospital."

"How can that be? He was so optimistic. How could he do this to me? I could give birth any day!"

"Don't panic," Tammy assures me across the telephone wires. "I'll figure something out. Let me make a few phone calls."

My husband echoes the "don't worry" mantra. This was also his song to me during my first pregnancy, when, with my very active fetus, I was sure Meira had at least two heads, ten arms, and twenty legs. I was constantly asking him, "Are you sure she's okay?"

"She's fine, she's just fine," he told me. "Besides, Jews always think positive." I knew his global assurance might not have been one hundred percent historically accurate. But at the time it comforted me. Thinking back, it was probably an unconscious association with my grandmother's positive outlook, delivered through the umbilical cord of the Jewish people.

Now, though, I couldn't help but indulge myself in a ride through the haunted house of my anxiety. I paced (or waddled) back and forth on our stone kitchen floor. "Don't worry? How can I not worry? Will another doctor be willing to assist me in a natural birth? Will he be willing to take me as a patient in my ninth month?"

"Tammy said she'd find someone, so she'll find someone." I hear him walk off mumbling something about those "darn pregnancy hormones," and I am left alone to ride out the waves of my anxiety.

Despite my doubts, as my husband predicted, Tammy comes through. This time, it is she who is delivering me a gift.

"Okay, Ellen, I've got good news and bad news." At the prospect of bad news, my mental ghosts hoist their haughty capes to taunt me, and spread themselves like a barrier across the door of hope and possibility.

"Okay Tammy, what's the bad news?"

"Well, it seems that Dr. Frank's departure has created a huge political rift in the hospital. He was forced to resign after being accused of allowing a VBAC on a questionable patient. Anyway, the medical director is furious with him because of his unconventional medical practices, and because of the fact that he wouldn't resign voluntarily. The fallout of all this is that none of the other doctors will take you on as their patient."

I hold on to the phone, too angry and stunned to respond. "Ellen, are you there?"

"Yeah, I'm here. So what's the good news?"

Tammy doesn't skip a beat. "Would you consider having a midwife deliver you?"

"A midwife? A midwife to assist in a VBAC? And what will she do if something goes wrong?"

She responds as only Tammy can, with a confident, authoritative voice, which is yet as gentle and innocent as the new life itself. I can almost feel her hand reach out from the receiver to touch me. "Ellen, I have a very competent midwife in mind. Her name is Ilana Shemesh, and there is a doctor who has agreed to be her backup."

Ilana agrees to meet with me the next day, as there is no time to lose. Not only might I give birth early, but also falling into the hands of a staff doctor boosts the chances of having a C-section. Seated at a small hospital desk, Ilana's long, delicate face wears the tired expression of one who has attended an all-night birth. I tell her that I'm thankful she had time to meet with me.

She smiles in acknowledgment, and returns her focus to my infamous medical records. She reads aloud: " 'December 8, 1993, 8:30 p.m. Medical Entry. Thirty-six hours PROM [prolonged rupture of membranes, i.e., water breaking], patient making fair efforts of pushing, no progress. Baby stuck in deep transverse arrest' — Wait a minute, baby stuck in deep transverse arrest?

That's no medical reason for a C-section. I see no reason why this baby can't be delivered naturally."

I'm astounded to hear her echo Dr. Frank's reaction and confirm his medical opinion. More sure than ever, I take each one by the hand, put one foot in front of the other, and, holding onto Grandma's present, I walk to the metaphorical door. I am ready to walk through.

Before I leave the examining room, I feel a few painful twinges in my abdomen. Ilana hooks me up to a fetal monitor. No longer afraid of the whirring sound that testifies to my last agonizing defeat, she reads the needle markings as "probably false labor, probably nothing." I agree with her, since my due date is not for another two weeks, and wish her good night.

"Probably nothing" wakes me up at 5 a.m. They say there is a hormone that makes a woman forget the intense pain of labor; otherwise, there would be many more only-child families in the world. I count the contractions thirty seconds in duration and five to ten minutes apart; I know that I've got quite a while to go.

Later that morning, as my labor slowly advances, Tammy is by my side. I want to go inward, to retreat from this world of pain, as if to say, "Grandma, take your lousy present back; I'd rather do it Mommy's way." Tammy encourages me to fight back: "Don't close your eyes, look into mine." As I gaze into the serene glass pools of her eyes, I see hope, as she serenades me. The beautiful chassidic melody she hums transports me to a place of serenity.

It is noontime. Ilana arrives, as I am sure that I will be giving birth momentarily. Hours pass. I am getting frustrated. We walk upstairs and downstairs. David orders pizza for everyone. I can't eat. David goes back to work. I can't sit, or walk, or pray. Ilana suggests checking me.

These internal exams are never pleasant, but the hope they will bring news of cervical progress gives me the stamina. She sighs as she removes the rubber gloves, "You're still four centimeters dilated." This is disheartening to me, and I plead for an epidural. But my ladies in attendance have been putting me off, as it might stop my labor. Ilana, thankfully, recognizes my deep need for rest, and we quickly prepare to leave for the hospital, where I am given an epidural (read: heaven).

That same evening, I am fully dilated. I still can't believe I will birth this baby naturally.

Pushing, pushing, pushing. Trying to bring this new life into the world, while my deepest fears and dreams push against each other in my soul. David is there rooting for me, absorbing my moans like a loving sponge. Tammy climbs up onto the hospital bed and tries to maneuver my legs, which are senseless from the epidural, into a newfangled birthing position. To no avail. I'm ready to close up shop, when Ilana calls out, "Look, I can see the baby's head!!" Still not absorbing it, I observe her walking in and out of the delivery room, opening up sterile packages containing huge gauze pads, syringes, and other sundry items I can't discern. "What are you doing, Ilana?"

"I'm busy getting the baby kit ready," she says, wheeling in the newborn bassinet. "You know you're going to have this baby in about five minutes!"

"What?" I manage to squeak out between pushes. "You mean I'm not going to have a C-section?"

She, Tammy, and my husband cannot hold back their laughter. "No, Ellen, too late for that."

Sure enough, not more than a few minutes later, I experience a sensation I've never felt before. There is a flash of life-sizzling pain, and I can barely register what is happening. David bursts into tears as he gazes on our seconds-old baby boy. "*Mazal tov!*" he cries out. I am having my own celebration as floodgates of joy, relief, and exhilaration open up to me.

Ilana readies the bassinet, and Tammy serenades the baby with a soul-awaking lullaby. As I nurse my baby for the first time and he draws life-sustaining milk from my body, an old door closes for me. Its closure buries the demons, the horrid memories of failure, and the terrible voices that want to keep me down. The doctor checks me: everything is intact.

Ilana helps me off the bed, as my whole lower body is still numb from the epidural. I watch her as she removes the sheets from the bed where I delivered a baby not half an hour ago. As I watch her wrap up the sheets, I symbolically wrap up the sense of failure that accompanied the aftermath of my C-section. I feel like I have finally birthed myself.

Two days later, I am released from the hospital. With my sweet baby boy nestling close to me, David and I have a few quiet moments alone. What with preparations for the bris, we've barely had time to celebrate.

"We did it," I tell him, as he parks the car outside our new home.

David turns and caresses the baby's cheek. "I know," he responds softly.

We were bringing home a baby in the Holy City of Jerusalem. Jerusalem, which means "city of peace, city of wholeness." Never before did I ever feel so whole and at peace, putting inner demons to rest, permitting myself to birth naturally. In His compassionate understanding, G-d sent me a skilled, understanding, and patient birth support team, and allowed me to be His partner in the most miraculous of all human endeavors. We name our baby Elchanan, meaning "G-d's merciful compassion," to reflect the ultimate spiritual gift we have received.

I Can

Michelle Smilowitz

Against the advice of most medical personnel, we chose to plan a home VBAC, an opportunity that is becoming very rare in America. Even hospital VBACs are fewer than ever, and only one doctor was willing to let me have a minimal "trial labor." Unfortunately, his success rate was not too encouraging. From the moment my first child was born, I believed that home was the safest place for me to have babies, and I trusted that this was indeed the best choice for my baby and me. I am convinced that if I had attempted a hospital birth and hadn't had such supportive care providers I would definitely have had yet another unnecessary cesarean.

This birth story really begins February 13, 2000, when my son Yitzy was born by cesarean. His birth was a planned-birth-center-turned-hospital birth (the birth center had a fire) with a group of certified nurse midwives. After a Bradley-educated pregnancy, I went into labor at 41 weeks. My doula-attended, unmedicated labor was about a day long and culminated in three hours of nonprogressing pushing, without any urge to do so.

At this point we were told that the baby was "too big" and might get badly injured in the birth, and so we agreed to a nonemergency cesarean. The baby weighed 9 pounds, 9 ounces.

This unwanted surgical birth was devastating, creating deep feelings of letdown, sadness, and depression. However, while Yitzy's birth was truly disappointing, it was also a wonderful opportunity for growth. It is, for me, a constant reminder that G-d rules the world and no matter how well one plans, in the end we are not in control. I spent the three years following it reading and learning, finding supportive peers (through ICAN, the International Cesarean Awareness Network), and becoming a doula. I also had the opportunity to become the leader of my local ICAN chapter, developing the tools to help other women recover from cesarean surgery and plan their subsequent births.

Meira's birth was the result of a many-day-long labor process, beginning on Monday and culminating with her birth at 2:06 p.m. on Thursday, April 10, 2003, four days before Pesach.

On Monday I woke up feeling "different"; I felt crampy and out of sorts, which was exactly how I remembered the feeling of early labor. I was excited — this could be the day — but didn't mention anything to my husband or my mom (who was staying with us at the time). At nine, I met my friend Miriam for our regular two-and-a-half mile walk around Seward Park. During the walk I felt one or two contractions that were more noticeable than the Braxton-Hicks I'd been having for weeks. Pesach was only a week away, which was a big source of stress. I was worried about planning a Pesach bris (in a city where both caterers were going on vacation). I also needed to finish my Pesach cleaning, but I was nervous to make the house completely ready, in case I would absolutely need to eat a piece of toast or a cracker in whatever room I had finished cleaning during the labor.

I spent Monday Pesach cleaning, with contractions coming a few times every hour. I was scheduled to have a biophysical profile at 4 p.m. (I was 41 weeks and 6 days), but I canceled it and went to the chiropractor instead. (I hadn't had any ultrasounds during the pregnancy and really didn't want to have one now, figuring I was about to have the baby.) Not pleased with this, my midwife insisted on a 42-week deadline for medical consultation.

At bedtime, contractions kicked in every fifteen minutes and continued throughout the night. I stayed lying down in bed, but jumped onto my hands and knees to deal with each contraction. This helped pass the night away — although some sleep would have been nice.

At around 5 a.m. on Tuesday morning, the contractions finally tapered off, but by about 6:30 I realized that I had had a show. I decided that today was the day, and asked my husband, Mark, to stay home from work. I didn't have as many contractions on Tuesday morning, and at noon we went for a walk to get things going.

We spoke to the midwife a few times during the day, and she expressed her concern. She pushed us to get a biophysical profile done right away and do something to "get things moving." We resigned ourselves to doing the biophysical profile. When I got off the phone with her, I burst out crying. I was uncomfortable with the idea of getting stuck in the medical system, and I wanted this baby to be born ultrasound free.

After calming me down, Mark called our midwife

back and explained that I was not ready for a biophysical that day but would be willing to do it the next day. He clarified with her what exactly were her concerns. After she listed them (baby size, presence of meconium, fluid, amount of fluid, and so on), he asked her point blank: at what point would she no longer agree to be our midwife? She said that she would tolerate four more days without doing something to move things along, and wanted me to promise to do the biophysical on Wednesday.

We agreed to these criteria — I was pretty convinced that I couldn't deal with these contractions for four more days without doing something, anyway! After this I was able to relax and again feel pleased about all of my birthing choices.

Contractions started again in earnest on Tuesday evening, and I had another relatively sleepless night of somewhat regular, painful contractions that didn't seem to progress.

On Wednesday, with the contractions tapering off again, I decided to walk with Miriam again to help get labor started. Now I was convinced that this was the day my baby would be born. Contractions continued throughout the day, but became farther apart. Both Mark and my mom went to do things during the day and I had one last day of just hanging around with Yitzy (but no nap!). I was so tired that at one point I told him I would only read to him if we were lying down.

At 3 p.m., Mark and I left to go to the chiropractor, and then we finally went for the much-avoided biophysical profile.

The test was fairly annoying because the technician refused to release any information to us (she said we had to ask our doctor), but by looking over her shoulder at the monitor I could tell that everything was more or less fine and that the baby was in perfect anterior, head-down position. I had a few contractions during the test, which was rather uncomfortable.

Rather than going straight home, Mark and I decided to go out for Chinese food for dinner. (I must admit wondering if this was something I wanted to throw up during labor.) Deciding that I couldn't deal with this off-and-on labor any longer, I made an appointment for an acupuncture treatment for the next day.

We arrived home at around seven, to find Yitzy fast asleep — this was my opportunity to take a warm bath. My contractions were becoming more and more intense. After consulting with my support team, we delayed ordering the birthing pool, and at midnight opted to try to sleep. Exhaustion had undermined my last birth, and I did not want that to happen again. Dragging myself from the bed after an hour's sleep, we bundled up, going outside into the still, crisp, night air. I faced the reality that maybe this was finally labor. Contractions suddenly started coming every two to four minutes, so, to everyone's relief, at 42 weeks and 2 days I called in the team.

Unexpected back pain during each contraction took me by surprise. The baby was in a good position, so what could it be? My doula arrived at about two-thirty. As we waited for the birthing pool to arrive, I labored in the bathtub to help the pain.

When it finally arrived, we realized it would take time to fill up, so I asked Mark to help by boiling water in large pots to fill it more quickly. We therefore fulfilled the traditional custom — or joke — of boiling water.

Finally, at around six I entered a full tub. It was a nice change of pace and a bit of a relief, but not the instant pain reliever I had expected.

Another disappointment was noticing that dark had become dawn, and my plan to go into labor during the still night and give birth before daybreak was dashed. My midwife and her assistant, who had arrived hours before without my even noticing, became more involved. After homeopathic remedies didn't seem to remove enough of the pain, I began pleading for an epidural. At this point I was glad to be home, since no one had an epidural to give me.

I remember moaning, "No, no, no" during contractions and feeling very discouraged, even saying, "I can't do this." This is where my midwife really stepped up. At some point between contractions, she looked at me and said, "Michelle, this is exactly what we talked about. You told me that at some point during labor you were going to try and quit, and I was going to have to turn around to you and tell you that you could do it. This is the point. Stop saying no, and start saying yes."

They helped me out of the tub and I maneuvered into different lunge positions. They took pressure off my back with a double hip squeeze, relieving my back pain.

Intermittently monitoring the baby, my midwife gently insisted on an examination. I screamed with joy to discover that I was fully dilated.

I was scared to push. I was afraid of the pain, afraid of failing, afraid the baby wouldn't come out, and afraid I would have another cesarean. I really resisted hard for a while, even though back pain did feel a bit better when I pushed. I wanted to quit, and kept asking to go home, or put things on pause, or come back and do this all another day. I also spent a lot of time asking, "How much longer?" like a little kid on a car trip.

Moving over to a hands-and-knees position, leaning

over a birthing stool made laboring easier.

Crowning was very intense until someone said, "The head is out." Meira entered the world with her hands next to her head (compound presentation, possibly the reason for this difficult labor). My head reeled with exhaustion coupled with disbelief, and my midwife told me, "Continue pushing when you are ready." After delivering the shoulders, I laughed with the delight of seeing my new baby girl and my accomplishment of bringing her here. I had always wanted a girl, but I was mainly happy that I wouldn't have to deal with the craziness of a Pesach bris — or a bar mitzvah in thirteen years' time! There was no need for stitches.

About twenty minutes after she was born, Yitzy and my mom almost danced into the room to see her. After his initial interest, Yitzy waned, more interested in the mouth-watering chocolate and vanilla ice cream birthday cake in the freezer. While he dug in, Mark and I made the phone calls to share our good news.

A Third Try

Sara Huberman

Let me take you on a journey that really started almost two years ago following my second birth, which was also my second cesarean.* From then on, there was always the thought at the back of my mind, *What will be the next time? Do I even have the option to try a birth from below? Is it safe? Should I bother?*

Thank G-d, shortly over a year passed and I was pregnant again, with mixed feelings. I was thrilled to be pregnant, but I was ambivalent about the roller coaster ahead of me. You know, that "here we go again…" kind of feeling. I knew that if I were allowed the opportunity, I would try my darnedest for a natural birth. However, there were so many unknowns; perhaps it would just be easier and much less complicated to go directly to the operating room?

As I neared the completion of my second trimester, I realized it was time to take action. Books, articles, and research on VBAC's were to be *the* major undertaking of the next three months. I knew in my heart that, even

---

* See "Big Head Facing the Wrong Way," p. 123.

with all the uncertainty, I would have to try with a healthy respect for the potential additional risks involved (and therefore improved *tefillos*).

The next step was finding a doctor who would take the case. That was actually a pretty simple task. I had a choice of two, Dr. A. and Dr. Z. The hospital where Dr. Z. practiced would not allow a VBAC.

So, with a prayer in my heart, I contacted Dr. A. Although he had an office twenty minutes from my home, the hospital with which he was affiliated was a good hour and a half away. (The nearby hospitals all had policies to my detriment.) The distance did not scare me — not with the long labors that I was used to! On examination, Dr. A. found nothing structurally unusual as far as he could tell. He told me to come back at the beginning of my ninth to check the thickness of the scar. Until then, (besides for holding my breath), I should watch my diet, specifically sugars, to keep this baby as small as I could, in order to boost my chances of a natural birth. So, with the help of a neighbor, I found a glycemic index diet, a healthy alternative to those protein-only diets, involving choosing your carbs instead of eliminating them.

After weeks of research, knowing that we potentially had a small chance — but still a chance — we decided to ask the advice of both doctors and *rabbanim*. I was still uncertain whether I wanted to hear a positive response, yet I dreaded a negative answer. We were given the go-ahead to try, with blessings, from the *rabbanim*.

Exercise and my special diet had kept my weight in check, and now my psychological gymnastics would be over with today's appointment to ascertain if the scar was thick enough. The verdict was in: the scar was sufficiently thick! The baby, however, changed from a perfectly anterior position to transverse. Thoughts of giving up started crossing my mind again, although I kept hearing my friend's voice saying, "This is your last chance. Do everything you can, so if it doesn't work you will have left no stone unturned."

Feeling some emotional exhaustion, we anyway began to do more *hishtadlus*. My husband went to visit the son of Dayan Fisher, *zt"l*. I booked an appointment with a chiropractor and righted all the *sefarim* (books) in the house.

The next day found me at the chiropractor's clinic. The first thing that he did was put that baby's head down. Yup! He just felt around my abdomen, found the head, and guided it to where it should be. (It took a few tries, as the baby would not stay still.) And then, he worked on my back and told me that I had a "stuck coccyx." Apparently, the coccyx, a generally stable part of the back, is supposed to move out of the way during labor, up to ninety degrees. And mine did not move. Not ten degrees. And so he manipulated until it did move. I was very relieved.

I was relieved, but not everybody else was. My husband (who was very supportive), my parents, my in-laws, were all nervous. Was I sure I was doing the right thing? From what they had heard it all sounded very scary. Mind you, I was very concerned, too, constantly second-guessing my decision. It helped, however, that I had approval from *rabbanim* who were familiar with the medical realities.

My due date was now only a couple days away, and a doctor's appointment showed all was well except for one thing…the baby's head was facing forward, a less than ideal position; the main reason for my previous cesarean. The positive news was that the baby seemed smaller than my daughters had been at birth.

I told my friend about the results, and she mentioned a woman named Esther Marilus who had been successful in moving her baby into a more optimal position. Wanting to do all the *hishtadlus* possible, I called her first thing in the morning. It wasn't just any morning — it was the Friday before Shabbos HaGadol. Without even a second's hesitation, Esther had me come over and, using ultrasound, twisted me and turned me into crazy positions that I didn't even pretend to understand. The cord had been wrapped in four places. It was released from one, and the head was now well engaged in a perfect anterior position. She sent me home, saying, "Take a warm bath to relax your body before contractions start."

There was a lot of movement on Shabbos, my estimated due date. I davened that the movement was the baby getting ready to come out.

Throughout Shabbos I was having inconsistent contractions and I tried to rest and relax, hoping nothing would happen on Shabbos. I picked up the phone as soon as I saw three stars. "*Shavua tov,* Dr. A. This is Sara." With some panic in my voice I updated him on the latest events and arranged to meet him in his office. In his calm manner, he checked me, did an ultrasound, and timed my contractions. "Relax. You still have a while ahead of you. Why don't you go home and get a good night's sleep. By tomorrow you'll be glad you rested." He left me with specific instructions about when to call.

As I was exhausted, I thought that was a great idea. The contractions settled down, and I showered and crawled into bed. And then...wham! The first one hit. Somewhere between eight to ten minutes later...wham! Another one hit. There was no way I was going to sleep tonight. Wham! There went another. They were finally consistent, but not quite fast enough. They kind of hung around eight minutes apart. I filled the bath and settled in. It looked like they were coming seven minutes apart. Time to call the doctor.

I climbed out of the bath and waited for the contractions to come even closer together, but they slowed down! I whispered some prayers and went back to bed. My brain was reeling throughout. *Was this the right thing to do? Will I go through all this pain again — for naught?* But I had to try.

Wham! *How am I going to handle the drive to the hospital like this? Should I give up?*

Finally, my husband decided that, regardless of the magic number seven, it was time to call the doctor. I called my parents to pray for me and called the babysitter to watch the kids. As soon as I started making these phone calls and moved out of my forced relaxed state, the contractions sped up, very quickly. Dr. A. arrived soon after and checked me. "Well," he said, with a bemused look on his face, "you're almost fully dilated."

"I'm what? What does that mean?"

"It means that we're not making it to my hospital."

Silence.

On the way to the closest hospital, my waters opened. Feeling intense pressure, my elation that it was going so quickly mingled with panic that my doctor wasn't going to be the one to help with the delivery itself.

When I arrived, my labor coach worked with the staff to allow me to deliver standing in an open pelvis stance. The quick birth I had while in this position took everyone by surprise, with the midwife barely slipping into her gloves. There was no time for the usual questions, only the delivery of my bright-redheaded son, weighing in much less than my girls. The roller coaster ride was over (at least until the next time)!

FYI...

For further information on VBACs, see G.A. Macones, et al., "Obstetric Outcomes in Women with Two Prior Cesareans; Is Vaginal Birth after a Cesarean a Viable Option?" *American Journal of Obstetric Gynecology*, vol. 192, no. 4 (April 2005), pp. 1223–1228, and A.B. Caughey, et al., "Rate of Uterine Rupture during a Trial of Women with One or Two Prior Cesarean Deliveries," *American Journal of Obstetric Gynecology*, vol. 181, no. 4 (October 1999), pp. 872–876.

Another Way to Handle It

Birth #11

Sima Spetner

Week 41. Baby over 8.5 pounds. Biggest till now was eight pounds. Blood pressure rising: 165/110. Nervous doctor (I understood him). I was being sent to the hospital.

Day One

5:00 p.m. They decided to sweep (or strip) the membranes to stimulate labor.

9:00 p.m. Nothing happening. "I have ten children at home," I cry. I am not yet prepared to have a cesarean.

The hospital staff, not wanting to take responsibility for inducing me, since this was my eleventh birth, said, "An induction is too dangerous for you." "Not worth the risk." "Think of your family."

I understood them as I did the doctor, but a cesarean is not a simple thing — it's major surgery. And recovering with ten other souls to take care of would not be easy. I wanted to be sure it was necessary.

I decided to hire a senior doctor privately, who

would not panic but would follow my progress carefully.

Dr. Cohen looked over my file, then heard my concerns. At last he told me, "Go home, relax, and take drops to reduce your blood pressure. And, Sima, be back at 6:30 a.m. sharp."

After a great night's sleep, despite some worried thoughts as my head hit the pillow, we were at the hospital at 6:30 sharp.

Day Two

"Good morning," says Dr. Cohen, looking as if he also had a fitful sleep. "I want to insert some suppository gel (prostaglandin). Then we'll wait six hours and see if labor begins."

"Okay," I responded, having total faith in his judgment.

7:30 a.m... 8:30 a.m... 9:30 a.m. 2:00 p.m... Nothing.

"We're going to do this a second time," he announces to the new midwife, as the shift has just changed.

4:00 p.m... 5:00 p.m... 6:00 p.m... 9:00 p.m. and nothing. At least the midwife and I had some nice chats and even a light dinner together.

"Go home. Get a good night's sleep," says Dr. Cohen. I said good night to him and to the staff I was getting to know.

"See you tomorrow," said two of the midwives who were going to be working the afternoon shift.

Day Three

6:30 a.m. "Hello," I chirped, feeling great, since every day my blood pressure stayed stable, albeit high, and Dr. Cohen was allowing me to try a birth from below.

Today was different. "We're going to try a slow dose of Pitocin," I was informed.

"Whatever you say, Dr. Cohen."

"How are you?" welcomed the 7:00 a.m. staff, some of whom saw me two days previously.

"Great," I responded, "as long as the baby and I are fine."

The Pitocin was slowly increased during the day, but nothing was starting. By 10 p.m., with my blood pressure up to 185/110, I said good-bye to the evening shift, some of whom I now knew by name. Dr. Cohen sent me to the ward for some overnight observation.

Day Four

By now some of the midwives were bringing in family pictures to show me.

7:00 a.m. Dr. Cohen decided to try Pitocin again, raising the dose.

1:00 p.m. Some slight fetal distress. "Okay, depending on how the baby copes, we may have only two options: a cesarean, or a higher dose of Pitocin to bring the birth quickly. It isn't serious, but it needs continual supervision."

"I think I can handle more Pitocin," I answered meekly.

After one and a half intense hours beyond belief, I opened to nine and a half centimeters.

It was 2:35 p.m. "The baby is descending, but there is now serious fetal distress. He has to come out now!" exclaimed Dr. Cohen matter-of-factly.

I reached full dilation within five minutes, and a

vacuum assisted my little *meidele* into this world. The cord was wrapped three times around her neck and had tightened as the baby descended. She screamed immediately and had a perfect five-minute Apgar score.

When the shift changed once again, a new midwife entered. When she saw me, she said, "You're still here?"

"Yes," I replied, "but I gave birth!" (The staff had taken the baby to the nursery for supervision.)

"Oh, no!" she cried. "I lost the bet!"

"What bet?" I questioned.

"The whole staff was betting if you would have a natural birth or cesarean. I was sure you would end up having a cesarean! *Mazal tov* anyway! I am so happy for you."

We laughed together and then she offered, "Would you like a cup of tea?"

What was really special was that two days later, before I left the hospital, the nurses and midwives presented me with a beautiful layette, complete with baby clothes and paraphernalia. And guess what paid for it? The money from the happy losers of the bet.

Challenges

Nechama S.

If G-d does not build the house, in vain do the workers build. If G-d does not guard the city, in vain do the guards watch over it.

(Psalms 127:1)

*E*very pregnancy and every birth — creation in its purest form — is out of our hands. But, in this case, I was time and time again made acutely aware of Who was in charge, despite all the *hishtadlus* I put in during the nine months of challenges I faced.

When I became pregnant around Pesach, with the younger of my two children less than five months old, we were anticipating a challenging few months. Morning sickness, as in the previous two pregnancies, created a need for support that my neighbors were unable to provide. Even though I had moved to Israel and become a mother far from family, I had yet to know how challenging the next nine months would be.

By seven weeks, my stomach was so sensitive I started wearing my loosest clothing, shortly after followed by maternity clothes.

Challenge #1: My husband was starting a new job which required lots of preparation in the fall.

Challenge #2: We were moving from a rental to our own apartment, bought in a different community.

Challenge #3: At about ten weeks into the pregnancy, late on a Friday morning, I saw blood.

My midwife, Joyce, said to get examined. My general practitioner said, "You could go to the hospital. If you're bleeding heavily, they'll give you a D and C, and if not, they'll send you home." My rabbi's wife helped with spiritual strengthening and practical advice on what to do with the kids. Friends helped with childcare for our two-year-old, while my husband decided to take the baby with us to the hospital. We took some Shabbos provisions, just in case, as well as diapers, wipes, and formula.

Nothing amiss could be seen on the ultrasound, so, given the choice of staying in the hospital or going home to rest, I chose the latter. I was now on what is called in English, uninformatively, "bed rest." In Hebrew, the term used is *shemirat herayon*, or simply *shemirah*, literally, "guarding a pregnancy" — a term that reflects the Jewish attitude toward the importance and value of every pregnancy.

A "threatened miscarriage" — such scary words. The doctors said to rest as much as possible and "let's see what happens." Not so easy with a two-year-old and a seven-month-old, but I rested as much as I could. Our oldest continued to attend his playgroup, while the baby went out every morning to a babysitter who was recommended by a friend. She was a real gift from Heaven, writing little notes about what our precious little one was up to.

Forced vacation was okay until boredom and frustration began to set in. There were so many questions: What could I do? What was too much? Who would take care of the kids in the afternoons? How long would I have to be on bed rest? How would we get packed for the move? And, most of all, what would happen with this pregnancy, this baby?

I was taken off bed rest long enough to look for furniture, when the same cause of my first bed rest put me back in bed again. During this time, I went for more ultrasounds and the source of the bleeding was found: the sac had separated from the uterus. I was told to continue resting and hopefully the gap would close. The second ultrasound showed it had closed somewhat, and thank G-d, the third showed no separation at all.

I had spoken with Joyce, who told me that this situation was not a contraindication for a home birth, and that after the separation healed, there would be no impact or effect on the rest of the pregnancy or the birth. We were quite relieved to be past the uncertainty of the last few months and started to feel that we could now move on to dealing with the challenges of adjusting to a new home, a new community, and a new job. However, G-d had other plans.

It was October when I finally got around to getting the routine blood tests Joyce had requested before the threatened miscarriage. We had moved, finished some renovations on our new home, and made it through the High Holidays, and my husband had started his new job. After having seen my test results, My obstetrician, Dr. S., asked me to make an appointment to come in and see him. It sounded ominous. I found myself in his office two days later, hearing that the CMV test had come back positive. The fourth and biggest challenge: CMV. I didn't know anything about cytomegalovirus then, but I was to learn quite a bit about it in the next few months.

Dr. S. was curious why I had done the test. I explained it was part of the homebirth midwife's requested tests. I then remembered that I had not been feeling well when we moved, with fatigue and a sore throat. When I saw the doctor then, he told me I had a case of "motheritis"; exhaustion from raising two small children, being twenty-two weeks pregnant, and moving.

CMV, depending on when the mother catches it and the reaction of the fetus, can cause an enlarged liver and spleen, brain damage, hearing and vision problems, or stillbirth, G-d forbid. The majority of babies are healthy, but there is a wide range of possible effects. My gynecologist, Dr. F., sent me for a detailed ultrasound and told me to speak with a specialist in CMV. I also asked Dr. F. about my planned home birth. Although he was usually supportive of home births, in this case he advised against it.

The specialist's first available appointment was two weeks before my due date. After making many calls, I was able to get an appointment with a different expert for the following week. I arrived at the clinic only to discover that they were to give me a basic ultrasound, which was worthless for my purpose. Now I had to figure out the bureaucratic angle: getting the right papers, the right kind of appointment, and go again. My nerves were really jangled at this point, but my prayers reached an even greater intensity.

At last I went back to get the right ultrasound. *Baruch Hashem*, everything looked fine, but then the doctor wanted to check again after the baby moved, so he told me to go eat something sugary, walk around for a few minutes, and come back. After an ice cream (an unheard-of treat with my strict, low-sugar pregnancy diet) and a brief walk, I waited another forty-five minutes or so while he saw several other people who had come in after me. I kept thinking, *If I have to suffer with this baby, please let it be with multiple trips and hassles, an unpleasant doctor, and long, annoying waits. Please G-d, just make this baby whole and healthy.*

Finally, the doctor checked me again and everything appeared normal (such beautiful words!). The doctor could detect no signs of CMV. Although there are possible effects that cannot be detected with an ultrasound, most are detectable.

With the ultrasound hurdle behind us, we now had to decide where to have this baby. I was too far into my pregnancy to register at the most flexible, natural-birth-friendly hospital. I was worried, because my first birth, when I had been semisitting in bed with a monitor for many hours, had only progressed with large amounts of Pitocin. Even then, the baby had not descended until I sat on my knees and pushed for all I was worth. My second birth had stalled every time I lay down, and only progressed when I stood up and walked around. In the end, both babies were born naturally, thanks to my patience and the upright-labor thinking of my private doctor (birth #1) and my home-birth midwife (birth #2).

I was concerned that, as I was labeled high risk (because of the CMV), I might have less freedom of movement in this birth, with continuous monitoring. If this third birth followed the pattern of my previous two, restricting my movement was a bad option, to say the least. Multiple research shows that not only does continuous EFM not improve outcomes for babies or mothers, but it also increases the rate of instrumental deliveries and cesareans.

I anxiously awaited the meeting with the specialist, Dr. B., to get more information about the possible effects of the CMV both on our baby and on the birth process. I planned out my questions with the aid of my husband and midwife. Then I got a call: all of that day's appointments of that day were canceled, and I would have to reschedule. Another week of waiting and praying. Finally, the day came and my husband and I went to meet the specialist. We arrived on time, only to find a line of people waiting for her. There was at least half an hour of appointments before ours.

I was too nervous to sit still and my husband was hungry, so we went down the block to get him something to eat. When we returned to the doctor's office, the specialist had arrived, thank G-d, and we only had to wait through another two appointments before we were seen.

After Dr. B. apologized for the delay, we explained the situation to her. The first think she said was that if we had come earlier in the pregnancy she would have recommended termination (!). Then she recommended an amniocentesis. We rejected this option because it carries a 0.5 percent risk of miscarriage and would not have given any information that would have enabled us to help the baby. Finally, Dr. B. said there was a 40–50 percent chance that the CMV had not any ill effects on the fetus. Since the ultrasound had not found any liver or spleen damage, the probable areas of potential problems were the brain and hearing. She then gave us the name of an expert pediatrician to contact to examine the baby after birth.

Finally I had a chance to ask the doctor about having a home birth. It turned out that she was against home births in general, and, since we had a special issue, all the more so. Because her opinion seemed based on a negative attitude toward home birth in general, rather than on real concerns for our particular situation, I asked her what special considerations there might be in our case. The doctor explained that the CMV hazard would not make any differences in the birth, but it meant that the baby would need to be examined right away and its urine checked for CMV.

Since we had planned to have the baby examined by a pediatrician within twenty-four hours in any case, I wanted to know if the baby truly needed to be examined immediately after births or if the doctor was overexaggerating. I asked her, "Would I be able to hold the baby for a while before examination, to bond with him?"

"If the baby seems normal after delivery, the examination is not urgent," the doctor responded.

Now we had more information to discuss with Joyce. She had also discussed the situation with some expert doctors, and they had come to the conclusion that since all the prenatal tests had come back normal, there was no additional risk in a home birth. Everyone's concerns centered on what would be after the birth, and there was no indication of an effect on the birth itself or immediately afterward.

We live within ten minutes of a major hospital, where we could go in an emergency. Our midwife was also extremely experienced, having delivered thousands of babies over more than twenty years, both in various hospitals and at home. She had delivered my second baby, and I felt completely comfortable in her hands. But was my situation this time too risky to consider a second home birth?

This decision was too big to make on our own — we

needed to ask our *rav*. I spoke with our *rav*, telling him the medical information, including the doctors' and midwife's opinions. We shared our concerns about the hospital and our reasons for wanting a home birth. He told us that we could have the baby at home, but we had to be on alert in case the baby had to go to the hospital immediately.

Relieved to have the decision made, the drama behind me, I took a deep breath, put the pregnancy on the back burner and turned my attention to other things like driving lessons, checking out schools for my oldest, and catching up on housework.

Then again, maybe not. During a routine prenatal exam Joyce said she thought the baby might be breech and recommended an ultrasound to check. Three weeks before my due date, the ultrasound showed the baby in a breech position. Challenge #5: If the baby would not turn, not only would there not be a home birth, but there would have to be a planned cesarian.

At such a late date, and with a large baby, there was little chance the baby would turn on his own; our main option to attempt to avoid a cesarian was to do an external cephalic version (ECV). If the ECV was successful, then we could have a regular birth; if it was not, then we would have a planned cesarian.

My doula and friend showed me some positions that helped six out of seven women turn their babies from breech position. So there I was, lying head down on a slanted ironing board, listening to music and praying that my baby turn without the hospital procedure. I reminded myself that G-d is in charge and that I was only doing my *hishtadlus* and how grateful we were that everything seemed to be fine with the baby. We also wondered if maybe there was a problem with the baby

Challenges

and this was G-d's way of ensuring a hospital birth.

With the failure of the home-turning, we made an appointment for an ECV on Monday morning. My doula came along, which made things much easier. She knew where to go, chatting with the nurses, midwives, and doctors, asking for our doctor, and finding out where we were supposed to go.

So there I lay in the hospital bed, trying not to be too scared, and drinking water so the ultrasound used during the version would be clearer. My husband was saying *Tehillim* and comforting me with his steady presence.

The doctor was busy, so we waited, worried, and prayed some more. Then he came and did an ultrasound; the baby was still breech. He came back to give me a shot of muscle relaxant, after which I had to lie on my back for a while until it took effect. More waiting. The doctor finally returned to check, and said he wanted to wait until the muscles were even more relaxed.

While I was holding back the urge to release my exploding bladder, the doctor returned for the final time. He checked the baby with the ultrasound and told me to relax (easy for him to say!). I held my doula's hand as the doctor touched my stomach. Realizing that I was grasping her hand too tightly, I relaxed my grip (and my stomach), taking deep breaths as the doctor manipulated the baby through my relaxed stomach and uterine muscles.

Baruch Hashem, the baby turned to a head-down position! The doctor made it look so simple and easy — it was like watching an artist capture a scene with a few quick offhand strokes. And it wasn't even painful, just somewhat uncomfortable.

Two weeks later. My due date was approaching and I was hoping to go into labor early. The baby was already pretty big, and besides, my brother was visiting from America and I wanted him to see the new baby.

On Wednesday night I started getting mild contractions. They were pretty regular for a few hours, and then stopped.

On Thursday evening, we got a babysitter and went out to dinner with my brother. The contractions started up again, but since the contractions were mild and my other labors were quite long, I figured we had plenty of time for our evening out. After a few hours they stopped — again.

On Friday I called my doula to discuss plans in case of a Shabbos labor, but she said she didn't think this baby was coming on Shabbos. She was technically correct. In any case, I was not concerned about reaching her, since she lives only one street over.

Friday evening I had regular, mild contractions that lasted through the night. In the morning, I asked my husband to get my doula on his way to shul. By the time she came over at around eight, the contractions had stopped again. She waited around for a bit, chatting, and then left her supplies at our house and went home.

We had Shabbos lunch at our rabbi's home, and then went home to relax a bit. I woke up from a short nap with contractions that were increasing in strength. It was time for my husband to bring the kids to our friends and go get my doula.

It was 4:30 p.m. when my doula arrived. Her presence was very comforting. I tried not to fight the labor, the contractions, the pain. Instead, I focused on giving up control, accepting the contractions and pain. I sat on my doula's birthing ball, watching the sun set out the window of our balcony. After about half an hour, we decided that this was serious labor and it was time to contact my midwife, Joyce.

When Joyce first examined me, I was already quite open, and labor progressed quickly from there.

I don't remember much of transition, but I remember the urge to push. My doula put her hand on my shoulder as I pushed and the midwife regulated the pushing. A few minutes later the midwife said, "Don't push!" and I felt an intense burning sensation. Crowning!

And then…out came the baby! The midwife put him directly on my stomach. "Don't pull him closer up, the cord is short."

There he lay on my stomach, wet and beautiful. After the cord stopped pulsing, my doula cut the cord, and at last I got to hold my beautiful baby boy. The midwife put a bag on him to take a urine sample for the CMV test. She weighed him in a special hammock scale.

Later would come doctor's visits and an overnight stay in the hospital for various tests. But for now, I was holding and nursing my perfect baby. Thank G-d.

The many challenges in this pregnancy reminded me over and over again that Hashem is in charge. I needed to do the research, find a good caregiver, and use medical technology when necessary — but at the end of the day, everything is really in His very good, very loving hands.

FYI…

In home birth studies on thousands of women with uncomplicated pregnancies from England, Holland, Germany, and the World Health Organization, the mortality and morbidity of infants was the same or much lower in home births than it was in uncomplicated hospital births.

In a study of the *American Journal of Public Health* (March 1992), over two thousand women who gave birth at home were matched with a similar number of women who had hospital births. In the latter there was six times the amount of fetal distress, three times the amount of hemorrhaging, nine times the amount of episiotomies, more use of forceps, more cesareans, and so on.

In a study of 5,418 women in the *British Medical Journal* in 2005, similar statistics appeared.

(It should be noted that despite these dismal statistics, some hospitals and caregivers are making important strides in improving their approach to childbirth and should be commended on this.)

In Israel, home birth is legal but not the accepted practice. Less than 1 percent of women choose this option, but the numbers are rising steadily. Last year, there were three hundred home births in Israel by licensed midwives. Unlicensed and lay midwives probably did another fifty.

Home birth books from England and the United States are well worth the read. For more information on home birth in Israel, see Ilana Shemesh's website, www.birthathome.co.il.

(For more on ECV, see note on p. 180.)

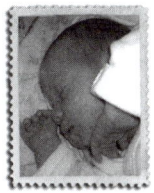

My New Sofa

Mindy Winter

Not all home births are intentional. My fourth baby made her way into the world in a way that none of us expected, but, as the songwriter said, "she did it her way."

It was a hot July, but seemed hotter as a result of my being past my estimated due date (EDD). Every time I left home, I felt self-conscious, wondering if some Greenpeace activist would try to push me back out to sea. To make matters worse, my husband, Dovid, was nervous about my being "overdue." He was born three weeks early and has been running about three weeks early ever since.

Every day that passed, he encouraged me to walk up hills, try different *segulah*s, and do something — anything. By the time I was eleven days overdue, he was beside himself.

Truth be told, I wanted to give birth, too, but as awkward and fat as I felt, I realized that few women make it to their eleventh month, and the baby would come eventually. But Dovid, being desperate, discovered yet two more ways to get out an "overdue" baby.

Late that evening, I yielded, agreeing to try.

The first thing he wanted me to do was drink one ounce of castor oil. The second involved mixing 150cc of fresh mother's milk with the white of one egg and drinking it. After an hour without results, my husband prevailed on me, "Drink one more ounce of castor oil."

By this point it was 12:30 a.m., and while Dovid went to sleep, I began reacting to the castor oil with the worst diarrhea of my life. I was so angry I almost vowed that if I ever went into labor, I wouldn't even tell him. The diarrhea stopped at around 4:00 a.m., but the cramps continued. It suddenly occurred to me that maybe I really was in labor, after all. I decided to wake my husband.

"Honey," I said, "I think I'm in labor."

He rolled over and said, "Great. If you don't need me right now, can you wake me later? You always have long labors anyway."

"No, wake up now. The pain is really strong. I think it's happening soon. I think we should get to the hospital. Get the kids dressed." He got them dressed in ten minutes flat while I was dealing with contractions coming every couple of minutes. The two oldest started giggling, imitating my moans. "Please get them out of here," I said. By now the contractions were almost nonstop.

We had eight different neighbors who had generously offered to take our three kids when the day would arrive. We thought it would be easy. I heard him phoning all the neighbors who had generously offered, "Bring the kids, any time of day or night..." and leaving desperate messages like "Are you there? Please pick up, it's the Winters. My wife is in labor; you said any time of day or night. It's 4:30 a.m. Please pick up!" None of the neighbors picked up the phone. After a few minutes,

Dovid started knocking on doors in our building. "OPEN UP! IT'S ME. I NEED YOU!!"

Do people really sleep so soundly? Finally a droopy-eyed man opened his door. My husband almost shoved the kids into his house. Turning to leave, Dovid shouted, "My wife's having a baby. Thank you so much."

Returning to me, he found me not coping. My breathing was out of control. I was so overwhelmed by the speed and intensity of this labor that when I got on to my sofa I didn't even remember to cover it with plastic. Suddenly my waters opened. This was a first! In my three previous labors I had an amniotomy at some point while pushing. I had begun to wonder if my amniotic sacs were really plastic bags. Now there was water everywhere.

"I'm not going to the hospital. I'm giving birth right here!"

Dovid was not his usual calm self. This was not what he had intended. First he called Magen David Adom to send an ambulance. Then he went to a neighbor to get help in the interim, hoping this time she would hear the banging on the door. The funny thing was that this neighbor herself had accidentally given birth at home a few years previously, and I had been present, despite my total inexperience at the time. Now the tables were turned. Between moans, I managed to look at her and say, "Talk about fair play."

Within a few minutes, the paramedics arrived. I was pushing as they came in. In front was a short, heavy-set man with a moustache, followed by a taller, quieter man. All I could think was, *I don't believe it. I have Laurel and Hardy as my birth attendants.*

As "Laurel" tried calming me with soothing words, his friend "Hardy" was opening sterile packages. He opened everything he had in his sterile birth kit. For days afterwards, Dovid found scalpels, umbilical clips, and pieces of gauze of varying sizes all over the living room.

Dovid was in the kitchen saying the twentieth chapter of *Tehillim*. It is a *segulah* to say this chapter twelve times while a woman is in labor. After saying a few *pesukim*, he gave up and started repeating with great emotion, "Hashem, help me. Hashem, help me. Hashem..."

My sofa is getting ruined, but maybe this will be my chance to buy a new one, was the crazy thought running through my mind.

Finally the baby's shoulders slid out. Thirty minutes after I realized I was in labor, it was over! I had an 8-pound, 3-ounce baby girl with fat cheeks and a head full of hair.

Sitting up and looking down at my ruined sofa, I worried out loud, "Hope now we'll be able to afford a new sofa." The paramedics whisked me to the hospital, where the nurses caught the placenta as it slid out. No pushing on my stomach this time — yeah! A cup of extra sweet tea raised my low blood pressure, and then I began nursing my new princess.

My accidental home birth gave me a lot of self-confidence and a beautiful daughter. But, in truth, I should add that it gave me one more gift. The paramedics called the next day to say *mazal tov* and...they took up a collection in Magen David Adom to buy me a new sofa!

FYI...

Castor oil should be used with caution, as it can be very effective. It should not be taken in conjunction with mother's milk, which has a high hormone content. Only if after a few hours you see that the castor oil hasn't been effective should you try something else.

Both these natural inductions usually help a woman to go into labor naturally, as it activates the oxytocin. This helps the majority of women avoid a Pitocin induction. However, these methods (as well as using herbs) should only be attempted under supervision of someone experienced with these methods.

If there is a need for a nonemergency induction, consider other natural alternatives such as reflexology, acupuncture, and chiropractic adjustment. All of these should also be done under supervision.

Above the Natural Order

Leeba Weinstein

As Jewish women we really are *mei'al hateva*, above nature. We are daughters of the King and, as royalty, we receive extra special measures of Hashem's loving-kindness.

Four of my six babies were breech. My first was a hospital breech; my second a double-footling hospital breech; my third was head down home-born; my fourth and fifth were breech, home-born. My sixth (at Purim 2006) was a posterior presentation, also born at home.

My very skilled doctor was especially trained for breech deliveries and had decades of experience.

The birth of my second child stands out for me as a prime example of *hashgachah peratis*. This is my story.

My parents were due to arrive from America on Friday afternoon. Since I was nine days postdate that day, my midwife recommended that I go to visit the doctor. My midwife and doctor worked as a team, a situation which freed up the doctor's time and left me comfortable with the skill and knowledge that comes from both.

I asked if the visit could wait until Sunday, and she agreed.

Once I arrived home, I happened to open up one of my all-time favorite midwifery books, *Hearts and Hands*,* to the section on postdate babies. Reading the information tipped the scales, and I went to the hospital to see my doctor. I wasn't too keen on going, but relying on my midwife's years of experience, as well as seeing the information in black and white, I decided to go.

The doctor said that everything was fine, but, to my surprise, I was about four centimeters dilated — without feeling any contractions! To our surprise, the baby was breech, so my doctor told me to come back in a few hours, just before Shabbos, to be checked again. We went home, packed a bag (just in case), and left our two-year-old with my mother-in-law.

A very kind and special family who lived a few blocks from the hospital opened their home for sleeping and meals to couples and their relatives who wanted to be close to the hospital on Shabbos. Feeling more secure five minutes from the hospital, we decided to stay with this family. We had been planning a home birth, but at this point decided to transfer to the hospital where everyone felt more comfortable. I was getting another lesson in the realization that flexibility in life is very important.

When my parents called from the airport wondering where we were, we explained the situation. Taxiing to Jerusalem, they also found themselves seated around this hospitable *chassidishe* family's Friday night table with my husband and me.

I was having mild, nonpainful contractions, so the doctor planned to come over every hour or so. The

---

* By Elizabeth Davis, published by Celestial Publishers in 1987.

steaming matzah ball soup and savory chicken dinner was occasionally interrupted by the doctor coming and checking my progress. When I was dilated about seven centimeters, my doctor said it was time to go to the hospital. He drove me there, while my husband, mother, and father followed on foot, as fast they could — out of sync with the stillness of the star-speckled summer's night.

They arrived to discover that my waters had just broken, finally causing contractions I could feel. Oh, right! This was how it felt the last time. "Wow, now it hurts!" I declared. Thankfully, this part wasn't long — maybe an hour or two.

My beautiful boy was a double footling (two feet first) breech, weighing about 8.5 pounds. He entered the world with one push.

Hodu laShem ki tov ki l'olam chasdo!

FYI...

By the 34th week, most babies turn to a head-down position. Approximately 3 percent are still in breech position at term. This makes delivery difficult (but in most cases possible) and is a cause for many cesareans.

There are different methods of turning a baby that is breech. External cephalic version (ECV) has an over 53-percent success rate for a first-time mom and a 75-percent success rate with others. If you want to try it, find a doctor who does it regularly and has a high success rate. It is done under ultrasound in a hospital setting.

If a baby is not footling breech (feet down) but rather bottom down, you can try an exercise called breech slant on an ironing board to turn the baby yourself. Do it with an empty stomach, putting light and music in the direction you want the baby to turn towards for about ten to fifteen minutes.

With Chinese medicine making a comeback, you can also try moxibustion with a licensed acupuncturist. This is a Chinese remedy from the mugwort plant, which is rolled into a stick and burned, then placed by the small toe to heat up the area in order to turn the breech.

There are *segulah*s to use as well.

Grandmom's Heart Revealed

What If?

Shari

Three and a half weeks ago, on October 18, at 5 a.m., I lost my dad here in Miami.

I had spent weeks at his side in the hospital and at his home, where he died. My daughter, who lives in Israel, and was expecting her second baby, had an estimated due date of October 14.

For weeks I discussed over and over with our *rav* what should be done *if*... What if my father is still in the hospital and Aviva gives birth? Should I go? Should I stay with my father? My brother said I should go — he would take care of Dad.

So many unknowns. What if he passed away and she gave birth during the shivah? Could I go? What if?... On October 19, we buried my father in New York by his mother's graveside. Aviva had still not given birth.

On the last night of shivah, at 9:30 p.m. Miami time, while I was sitting with my final visitors of the weeklong shivah, I got a call from Aviva. "Mommy, I want an epidural." I could hear the shaking in her voice and understood that she needed to get to the hospital right away, even though she said, "I'm not really ready to go.

You know I don't really want an epidural." She hadn't had one with the first, so there was an excellent chance she wouldn't have one now either. She must have been getting closer to the end.

"Call Tanta Sheindy (my sister, her doula) and get a taxi to the hospital right away," I said.

After the visitors left, I sat down in the kitchen with my *Tehillim*. The next call came shortly before midnight — a baby boy!

Eight hours later, the shivah ended, and my first stop was Shalom Travel for my ticket to Israel. My father's name, Avraham, was passed on in Jerusalem.

FYI...

In a recent study done at Brigham and Women's Hospital in Boston, 1,562 women were given an ultrasound upon admittance to the hospital, an ultrasound when an epidural was administered, and another ultrasound when they were close to full dilation. At the initial stages, the ultrasounds showed very little differences in the position of the baby. What was fascinating was that in the group of women who had been given an epidural, 12.9 percent of babies were in a posterior position (fetal head facing the spine of a woman's body; a problematic position) in the final stages. This in contrast with only 3.3 percent in the group who had not had an epidural.

The rate of forceps or vacuum and cesarean delivery was strongly dependent on fetal position (6.3 percent OA position [normal with face towards back]; 65 percent OP position [head down but facing forward]; 74 percent OT position [transverse lie of head]). Food for thought before taking that epidural.

The full study may be found in an article by Dr. Ellice Lieberman and colleagues, "Fetal Position during Labor and Their Association with Epidural Analgesia," *Obstetics and Gynecology*, vol. 105 (2005), pp. 974–982.

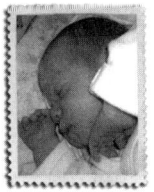

Tikkun

Chaya Newman

Twenty-eight years ago, when I became pregnant, I began to envision the type of birth that I hoped to have. My pregnancy was remarkably uneventful; I felt wonderful the entire nine months. I assumed that my labor and delivery would be the same. I expected to have the process go smoothly and quickly, enabling me to be back on my feet within a relatively short period of time.

I was in for a real surprise.

I had always wanted a natural childbirth. But, throughout twenty-one hours of labor with little progress and much pain, I found myself asking for painkillers, and even wanting a C-section. Our 7-pound, 3-ounce baby girl was born by cesarean. My condition was called "cephalopelvic disproportion." Our daughter had been too big to go through my birth canal. I was relieved that all was well, but I felt cheated out of a normal birth. Even though I understood that this was the way the birth had to end, I never made peace with it. I felt like I hadn't had a real birth.

Some twenty-one years later, our now married and

pregnant daughter called from her home in Israel. We were discussing the upcoming big event and the conversation turned to birth coaches (doulas). Calmly and respectfully, she told me that she had decided who she wanted to fill this position. "I know who I want," she said. "I want you!" Even though we were still living in the States at the time, I had planned to be in Israel over the summer. The tickets, however, were booked for the day our daughter was due. Knowing this information didn't deter her. In her course she had learned that only 5–7 percent of first-time moms give birth on their due date. She would wait for me to come.

As I hung up the phone, waves of panic washed over me. I was the one who got squeamish in hospital lobbies. I was the one who couldn't look when blood tests were being drawn. How was I ever going to stay conscious in a delivery room?

I posed these questions to a friend who had been her daughter's labor coach. She assured me I would be fine. Deep in my heart, I knew she was right. G-d would give me the strength I needed. Before I knew it, I was in Israel on that magical due date; the day the doctors said the baby would be born.

Our main concern now became preparing for the upcoming holiday of Shavuos. As we cooked the meals, we also prepared for any number of scenarios. What if we went into labor on these days? How would I know? Since the place where I was staying was a twelve-minute walk away from her house, we devised a system where she and her husband would leave a napkin in their door. If I arrived and saw the napkin, I would know to make my way to the hospital.

The holiday came and went. I never saw a napkin; there were no signs of labor. We continued to go about our daily affairs normally. Then, one morning, a week after her due date, our son-in-law answered my knock at the door and announced, "We might be in labor." We made the necessary calls, and a few hours later decided to go the hospital.

I watched our daughter with great pride and fondness. She was insistent on having as natural a birth as possible and made sure to communicate her ideas in a polite manner to all concerned. She walked, took showers, talked with her husband, spoke to G-d, and did not enter the labor and delivery room until the contractions were strong and hard. As she went through transition, the breathing techniques we had gone over came in handy. We worked together to focus her attention on the breathing rather than the pain as I wiped a cool washcloth over her sweaty face.

When it came to the actual delivery, a midwife took over. Even though I had never experienced the urge to push, now, twenty-one years later, I was overcome with the desire to push with my daughter and help her deliver her baby. With blessings from G-d, a healthy 8 pound, 4 ounce baby boy was born. What an incredible miracle!

There I stood, tears of joy streaming down my face, holding our first grandchild. It is a moment that will be forever etched in my memory. I felt so fortunate to be at this birth. For me, it was a *tikkun*, a rectification. I couldn't have the delivery I had hoped for, but I was able to assist our daughter in having the birth she wanted. As I experienced this birth vicariously, the disappointment and frustration I had felt for years all melted away and was transformed into healing.

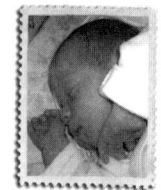

The Miami Induction

Briney's story

The call came an hour before Shabbos.

"Sarah, what should I do?"

"What's going on? Why are you calling so close to candle lighting?" I asked. Briney almost never called me with such anxiety in her voice. If anything, I was the one who would call her out of the blue, wanting some parenting advice or to be calmed down about a situation.

"Rochel [her daughter living in America] is going to be induced by Monday if she doesn't have the baby by then. Her doctor won't let her past the forty-first week. Her other two births were straightforward except that she took an epidural that she didn't want to take after postdate inductions, and now, with another induction hanging over her head, she's really nervous.

"Not only that, but her doctor won't take any responsibility for the baby if anything goes wrong. I mean, he could just continue to monitor the situation daily, so I don't understand the problem. Rochel doesn't want to change doctors now. It isn't so easy to switch doctors like it is in Israel if the doctor and patient aren't on the same page."

"Okay. Calm down, and we'll think this through," I said. We both took a deep breath and I said, "Get a pen and paper."

She returned to the phone, ready to write. I gave her the recipe:

> Take 4 tablespoons (2 ounces) of castor oil.
> Mix it with a cup of orange juice.
> Drink one third. After twenty minutes, drink another third. After twenty minutes, drink the last third. Stir well before drinking.

"If nothing happens before Monday morning," I continue, "have her drink this mixture and wait at home. G-d willing, something will start. If not, call me."

"Sounds gross," was Briney's reply.

"It doesn't have a bad taste, just a disgusting texture, and it works most of the time! And it's certainly safer and less painful than a Pitocin induction. Good luck and call me whenever you need to."

Tuesday morning:

"*Mazal tov!*" an excited voice bubbles on the other end of the phone.

"Briney, what happened?" I ask, mirroring her excitement.

"Rochel told her doctor yesterday that she wanted to take castor oil," Briney begins. "He said, 'Don't bother. It usually doesn't work and you'll just get a stomachache.' She said she was going to try anyway, since she was induced for the first two births and was petrified of being induced again.

"One hour after taking the castor oil concoction, Rochel ran to the bathroom with cramping and a running stomach. Suddenly, contractions began, strong and close. She told her husband to get her to the hospital, half an hour away. Twenty minutes into the drive he called a police escort, who told them to wait on the side while they called an ambulance. Rochel screamed, 'Just get me to the hospital!' The police immediately called the hospital to expect her. They got there less than five minutes later. Her husband got her into a wheelchair, and Rochel kept doing the 'blow, blow, blow,' to keep the baby in longer. They got to the labor ward just in time for the nurse to catch the baby."

When I called Rochel to wish her *mazal tov*, she was overwhelmed with gratitude. "That was such a wonderful experience. I barely felt the baby coming out, and the whole thing was over in two hours," she exclaimed.

"Were you okay with not having an epidural?" I asked.

"It was fine. I hated the inductions. The only thing I would do differently next time is take the castor oil in the bathroom in the hospital and wait there."

FYI...

There has been a serious rise in induction of labor, leading to major risks to the health of both mother and baby. I am therefore taking the liberty to write more than usual in this note.

There seems to be an overreaction to postdate pregnancies. There is also a pacifistic reaction of the mothers to agree to an induction when they have the right to decline.

According to the American College of Obstetrics and Gynecologists (ACOG) only 5 percent of babies arrive on their due date. With a primipara (first-time mom), the median pregnancy date is 41 weeks and 1 day. With second or more births (multiparas) it is 40 weeks and 3 days. It is obvious that the approach of induction at 41 weeks is not based on research or evidence. The research results state that there is no major difference in outcomes until past **43** weeks, and with daily monitoring the outcomes are the same.

For a pregnancy which is induced there is a higher rate of cesarean (double in first-time moms), uterine rupture (in multiparas), fetal distress, maternal hemorrhage, and more.

Synthetic oxytocin, unlike the natural oxytocin of labor, causes uterine contractions to come too close together, compromising the baby, and all too often leading to fetal distress. Also, the contractions are not in proportion to uterine dilation, therefore leading to "failure to progress" and very often cesareans.

Thus, induction is not an issue that should be taken lightly. Just like fruit on a tree, babies ripen at different stages. Rochel's three births all passed the forty-one-week deadline, which is a sign that either her cycle is longer, she conceives later, or the babies' gestational ages are longer.

Most *rabbanim* do not agree to induction unless there is a specific medical reason that could endanger mother or baby.

For a one-stop, in-depth research analysis of many studies on induction, consult *The Thinking Woman's Guide to a Better Birth* by Henci Goer (Berkeley Publishing Co., 1999), or S. M. Menticoglow and P. F. Hall, "Routine Induction of Labor at 41 Weeks Gestation: Nonsensous Consensous," *British Journal of Obstetrics and Gynecology*, vol. 109 (2002), pp. 485–491.

It's Not the Real Me

Bringing Home Joy
Anonymous

Postpartum Depression (PPD): a word I only became familiar with after baby #4. I had no idea what was going on inside of me, or that there might be a name for the heaviness I was experiencing. Despite having realized my dream of becoming the mother of four beautiful children, there was no joy in my role.

Our oldest was only four and I felt exhausted, overwhelmed by the constant demands of meeting their ongoing needs. All ambition had left me: I had no desire to tidy our home, take the kids to the park, or keep up my friendships. As children sometimes do, my children took advantage of my exhaustion, climbing up on the kitchen counters, making more mess. Encountering the crumbs from empty bags of pretzels or a broken egg on the floor left me feeling helplessly dizzy. Sometimes, it seemed the easiest thing to do was simply lie on the floor and reminisce about the pre-kids college days of my past.

Mechanically I fed, bathed, and clothed my older children and sent them off to kindergarten. My husband tried his best to help out, but he didn't understand what was happening to me. I felt so alone, isolated, guilt-ridden, and plagued by doubts about why I was not feeling fulfilled. I couldn't imagine a hopeful future.

Eventually, when my baby was more than three months old, my husband noticed an ad in a neighborhood newsletter that accurately described my symptoms. The ad announced a meeting for women with postpartum depression. I agreed to go.

There was a name for my condition! It wasn't merely psychological, but physiological. There were nurses and social workers at the meeting, and I finally had a glimpse of what was really happening to me.

Now that I knew what I was dealing with, I learned that there were herbs and medication that could treat PPD, and a friend told me who to contact. When I spoke to Miriam on the phone, she informed me that the St. John's Wort that she recommended would take about six weeks to start working.

"Six weeks!" I gasped. She then kindly offered to pay for a taxi, if I wanted to come to her home and begin treatment immediately. I found that I began to feel better within two weeks.

I read that many women who suffer from PPD find themselves afraid of future pregnancies, fearing the debilitation of postpartum depression. I, too, was very wary. "I want to have more children," I called out to G-d. "Please help me find the self that I lost somewhere along the way. Help me regain joy, laughter, and song!"

My husband and a few close friends helped tremendously with their supportive listening and acceptance of me as I was, never denying my feelings. Rabbis gave my husband ideas of how to proceed with our lives, including reading, classes, connection to a *rebbetzin* for emotional support, and other practical tips that follow.

I began an active process of examining and discovering which parts of myself were being neglected, and I re-evaluated everything that I was doing with my life. Realizing that I needed to get out more, I began doing some secretarial work and tutoring. The new contact with other teachers and meeting wonderful students was refreshing.

Mothering, my spiritual work, also needed to be evaluated. I found myself able to focus better on what were the most important tasks to me as a mother, and find ways to incorporate these inner discoveries into my daily routine. These were meaningful changes that made an enormous difference. My mothering and my self-esteem benefited tremendously from my reassessment. Dressing differently also gave me new confidence.

G-d answered my prayers. I regained my strength and sense of self. When our youngest was three years old, and I was expecting our fifth child, I prayed that G-d grant me the ability to care for my growing family. During this pregnancy, I had to spend a number of weeks on bed rest. I asked G-d that all would be well with our baby, so that we could serve Him with good health.

My due date came and went. Already in the forty-first week, I went for an afternoon nap. Startled awake by a contraction, I got up and washed my hands. As I was becoming more conscious, I realized that the contractions were coming at eight-minute intervals.

By the time I had finished dressing, called my husband to tell him to head home, and thrown together something for supper, the contractions were coming every five minutes! My husband's parents came to baby-sit, while we borrowed their car and sped off.

Now the contractions were every three minutes! I was breathing and yelling through the peak of every one, and my husband suggested stopping off at the ambulance station where his friend's wife had had an emergency birth. I was sure that we would make it to the hospital in time and insisted that he keep driving—fast!

By the time we arrived at the entrance to the hospital, I felt like pushing. My husband went to park the car, while I waddled rapidly past the guard, entered an open elevator, and pressed the number of the right floor. As soon as the door opened, I made my way into the first available delivery room I saw.

A nurse spotted me and asked, "Excuse me, where do you think you're going?"

"I'm having a baby!" I managed to reply.

She smiled patiently. "Well, you've come to the right place! Let me check you out and I'll assess how far along you are," she said, though her words seemed to come to me through a haze.

The room I was in was completely empty, except for one beanbag in the corner, which the nurse suggested I lean on while she quickly examined me.

When she checked me she was in for a surprise — my baby was already in the midst of being born! Five minutes after I entered the hospital, there I was, leaning on a giant beanbag, holding our newborn son! It was only then that I noticed that the place I had run into was a bare room! The maternity ward was undergoing renovations, and the beanbag was a sample of what was to be part of their natural birthing suite.

Suddenly, I heard my husband's voice calling from behind the closed door. "Are you in there?"

The stunned nurse called out, "Yes, it's a boy! Congratulations!"

My husband responded with shocked silence, assuming that there must have been a mistake. Then he asked again, "Are you in there?"

After the wrapped baby was nestled in my arms, we finally realized that we had forgotten to notify our doctor.

Only two hours earlier, I had been napping peacefully, unaware of any labor. It seemed to me that our newborn son's face shone with a glowing light. I sat gazing at him in my arms for hours after he was born, feeling an indescribably euphoric happiness at his arrival. I stayed awake all night, holding him, absorbing G-d's love for me. Those moments of blessed bliss made worthwhile all the previous difficulty I had experienced in my life. This incredibly delightful birth was a beautiful way for G-d to answer my prayers that our new baby bring joy, laughter, and song back into our lives and hearts!

When Yitzchak, which means "laughter," was a nursing baby, he suffered from a variety of allergies, which required me to stick to a very restricted diet. My husband and I didn't get much sleep during Yitzchak's first year of life, as he cried out from his discomfort. But incredibly, the more I gave of myself, caring for my baby, the greater grew our loving bond. Instead of resenting him and becoming despondent, I felt he was a treasured gift.

Yitzchak is now seven years old, with two younger sisters and a baby brother. As is natural when mothering eight children, there are times that are difficult, even days that are discouraging. Thankfully, I have learned effective ways to cope, and the love and joy that I always associated with being a mother is a part of my life. I look back at the period after my fourth child was born as I time when I was challenged to grow.

The postpartum depression that I dreaded would reappear has never returned. G-d has continued to bless us with the miracle of precious babies and the strength to care for them with laughter and love.

FYI...

As of yet, there is no research of the effect of St. John's Wort on nursing babies. In many situations, St. John's Wort can take too long to work. Medications can help sooner and more effectively without the stigma that used to be attached to PPD.

An extensive support system is very important for a mother suffering from PPD and even one who isn't, so that mom can have time to eat well and rest.

For more infomation on PPD, see Michal Finkelstein, CNM, *Delivery from Darkness,* soon to be published by Feldheim Publishers; Dunnewold and Sanford, *The Postpartum Survival Guide*, New Harbinger Publications, 1994; and Kleinman, MSW, and Raskin, MD, *This Isn't What I Expected: Overcoming Postpartum Depression*, Bantam Books, 1994.

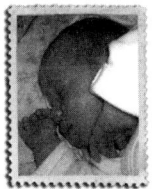

The Doctor Is In

Batya L. Ludman

Mr. and Mrs. L., both health professionals, thought they were well prepared for the arrival of their first child. Once through labor and delivery, the rest would be easy, they thought. They discovered they were very wrong. Breastfeeding was difficult and was not as "perfectly natural" as the books suggested. The baby lost weight, was very irritable, and rarely slept. Nothing was predictable, nothing went as expected, and nothing was a whole lot of fun. This was not how they thought it should be — what happened to those pictures of joyous, smiling couples looking down at a beautiful, happy baby? Didn't everyone say that having a new baby would be wonderful and one of the happiest events in their life? At the suggestion of their pediatrician, I was asked to become involved.

Mrs. D., the mother of two children under four, came to see me in the seventh month of her third pregnancy. This baby was unexpected, she'd had "difficulty" after her last pregnancy, and, already tearful, she wanted me to get to know her now so that I could help her later when the depression hit. She was not sure she would be able to handle it all again.

Postpartum blues, depression, or psychosis can take away all of the excitement one should feel at having just given birth and can turn a family's world into a nightmare. Often undiagnosed and underdiagnosed, many women suffer needlessly when help is really a phone call away. Let's see what each of these conditions entail.

Postpartum Blues

Postpartum or baby blues is very common, and affects up to eighty-five percent of women. It is seen as a mild form of depression that many women (especially new moms) experience after the birth of a baby. It usually starts a few days after delivery, peaks around three to five days after delivery and lasts a few days to a few weeks. Moms may appear sad, anxious, or irritable with no apparent cause. They may be moody, angry, overwhelmed, lacking energy, and unable to sleep. While feeling mildly depressed or somewhat out of control and helpless, these moms still look after their babies and function quite well.

First-time parents are sometimes disappointed to discover that their expectations about the perfect baby they visualize before birth may bear little resemblance to the reality after delivery. They are busier, feel less competent, and are often sleep-deprived. Coupled with hormonal changes of pregnancy, delivery, and breastfeeding, a mom may feel very much out of control and wish for the blissful "old days."

While it is perfectly normal to feel stress on many levels after childbirth, many a mom feels alone in her unhappiness. When involved early on, the role of the clinical psychologist or professional support person or group is to help the family make the transition to parenthood and realize that they are indeed "normal" and their stressful responses are normal. The new mom needs help in regaining a sense of control over those things she can control and needs to reduce sources of stress as much as possible. She may need practical support around the house, help with the baby, assistance with nursing, and general reassurance that she is doing everything right. Additional guidance in structuring her time and managing the various aspects of her life and her new family can give her a real sense of achievement as a new parent.

Postpartum Depression

Postpartum depression (PPD) is a more serious or severe form of the baby blues, affecting at least one in ten women. Often undiagnosed, it begins anywhere in the first year after delivery and may last from a few weeks to months. Symptoms may persist for six months or more and, if untreated, may worsen with many still being symptomatic a year later.

Unlike postpartum blues, a woman with PPD may have difficulty in looking after herself or her baby because of the severity of the depression. Symptoms of depression include, but are not limited to: severe mood swings, sleep difficulties, weight loss or gain, decreased energy, a sense of feeling trapped or unhappy, numbness, a desire to avoid socializing, lack of pleasure in life, lack of caring or concern for self or baby, a sense of despondency, trouble coping with and carrying out daily tasks, anxiety about the baby, panic attacks, confusion and forgetfulness, decreased sexual interest, feeling like a failure, hopelessness, suicidal thoughts, difficulty focusing or concentrating, difficulty making decisions, and somatic aches and pains.

While these are all signs of a moderate to severe depression, some of these symptoms — such as exhaustion and broken sleep, or a sense of feeling overwhelmed — are expected after childbirth, making them easy to ignore.

There is no single cause for PPD. Sleep deprivation is thought to be a contributing factor, and lack of support for the new mom will make things more difficult and demanding. An irritable, sleepless baby will put a parent under great stress. Hormonal factors, a change in brain chemicals, a drop in thyroid levels, a sense of loss on many levels after pregnancy, and a difficult and traumatic delivery and postnatal period can increase one's vulnerability to depression. Women with baby blues, a previous history of PPD, or a family history of emotional problems are thought to be at higher risk for depression. So are those who experienced a previous loss or who have other sources of stress in their lives, such as a move, an unplanned pregnancy, or not enough time between pregnancies.

This situation calls for immediate medical attention by a psychologist or psychiatrist to assess and treat the depression. The professional works with the mother, the father, and the rest of the family, sometimes alone or in combination with each other. Treatment for the mother is designed to alleviate or eliminate the depressive symptoms and stabilize her, helping her improve, recover, and prevent a reoccurrence. Treatment is focused on mobilizing the new mother and her resources, enabling her to see her strengths, make changes, and regain a sense of control in her life.

The professional may also provide developmental and parental guidance, teach parent-infant bonding activities and play skills, and give the mother reassurance with regard to parenting. Other techniques involve teaching relaxation exercises to help mom sleep and to impart a sense of calm and competency, examining irrational and unrealistic thoughts, positively reframing trouble areas, problem solving, and helping with communication issues for mom and dad, mom and parents, and mom and baby. Treatment might also include a referral to a new moms' parenting group which both educate and help mom to socialize with baby in a situation where she is with other new moms. A postpartum support group for mothers going through similar postpartum issues, where her specific needs are addressed and coping tools are acquired, is invaluable.

Depending on the severity of the depression, the professional may suggest a referral for medication as an adjunct (not a substitute) to the cognitive behavioral therapy that will be provided. Medication usually takes at least three to four weeks to begin to work, and some time may be needed to find the most suitable antidepressant. While it can be less, it may take three to six months before a patient feels better. PPD can have quite adverse effects on the baby's development as well as on the well-being of other family members — it is not only the mom who is at risk.

More Serious Disorders

Postpartum panic disorder, obsessive-compulsive disorder, and post-traumatic stress disorder are other conditions that may occur after birth, and although not dangerous, treatment is needed.

Postpartum psychosis and mania are severe, but rare, postpartum reactions. These reactions may begin days or weeks after delivery. They may come on dramatically and require hospitalization. Symptoms include extreme agitation and confusion, rapid and pressured thoughts, irrational thinking, severe mood swings, and harmful thoughts about oneself or the baby. Psychiatric treatment is urgent, because mother and baby may be at risk. Only afterwards will psychological care be helpful.

If you know of a friend or family member with postpartum difficulties, you would be helping her tremendously by encouraging her to seek professional help. Anyone showing symptoms of depression or anxiety during her pregnancy, crying and general unhappiness, or difficulty feeling good about the pregnancy, should discuss this with her midwife or physician. If a mother's adjustment seems at all beyond "normal," it is better for her to be seen professionally and be reassured and followed up, rather than wait endlessly in the hopes that it will just "go away."

New moms may require lots of assistance. They may be poorly equipped for "entering the trenches" and facing this new and very demanding job that requires twenty-four plus hours a day and tremendous flexibility. The rewards are limitless, but sometimes new parents have difficulty focusing on the positive, and realizing that each difficult stage really does end! Mom may need practical help and suggestions with many issues, including feeding, guilt, sleep schedules, and parenting in general. Most babies are far more difficult than one might expect, and getting to know and love a newborn takes time. Motherhood and breastfeeding are not completely instinctive — they have to be learned as well.

Friends can encourage mom to look after herself, eat, exercise, get out alone for a bit, and rest. Friends can also get involved by offering to baby-sit (so that mom can hop into the shower), help with chores, delegate some non-baby related tasks, drop over with a snack, and just be there to ensure that mom simplifies life and does only what needs to be done in order to take it easy. Sometimes, the hardest job a mother faces is learning to let things go a bit, to relinquish control and attempt to settle into her new life.

When a professional or support person is involved with the family she has a chance to see how parents deal with older children and how older children deal with the baby, and help the older child feel included while ensuring that his needs are met. Husband and wife can be encouraged to share feelings, talk to each other, and spend time alone as new parents. A friend or family member, can help a depressed mom understand the tremendous impact depression can have and, if these symptoms are noticed, you can help through the above practical advice and encourage the couple to seek assistance.

> *Dr. Batya L. Ludman is a licensed clinical psychologist in private practice in Ra'anana. She welcomes correspondence to ludman@netvision.net.il, or visit her website at http://go.to/drbatyaludman. She can also be reached by phone at 09-771-8815.*

FYI...

For further resources for postpartum depression, see Appendix B.

*For Fathers
by Fathers*

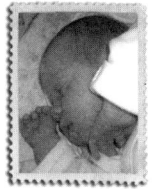

Men Are from Mars

Daniel Brody

My wife is a childbirth instructor. I find the subject to be both miraculous as well as fascinating. Since most of her classes consist of *chareidi* women, we decided that perhaps a class for men, given by a man, might be advantageous. I have been teaching men for a few years now, and it always amazes me how men are so different from women.

Forget the Aspirin

In John Gray's book, *Men Are from Mars, Women Are from Venus*, he describes how men and women are not only physically different, but they think differently, too. When most men encounter adversity, their natural reaction is to look toward solving the problem. He refers to men as "Mr. Fix-it." Most women, on the other hand, prefer empathy to get them through their crisis.

Take, for example, the case of Reuven. One day, Reuven trips on a broken stair right outside his front door. A woman's reaction to this incident might be,

"Oh, my! Are you all right?" On the other hand, a man's reaction might be: "You know, if you go to the local hardware store, you can pick up some sealant and fix that pretty easily."

Still doubtful? How about this scenario: When a man complains of a fever and headache to his wife, he might hear, "Oh, you poor dear, here, lie down. Can I get you some tea?" When a woman complains of a fever and headache to her husband, he will typically offer a "fix-it" suggestion like "Why don't you go to the doctor," or, "Why not take some aspirin?"

Now, you might be asking yourself, *Why does he start the class with this information?* The answer is simple. When it comes to labor, most men say to themselves, albeit subconsciously, "There is nothing for me to do here. This hospital is full of experts who know a whole lot more about childbirth than I do. There is nothing for me to fix." They look at labor as a medical problem, and not a natural process. And we all know that medical problems are left to the experts.

Now don't get me wrong. Doctors, nurses, and midwives do belong in a labor room, but labor is often a long process. The hospital personnel are usually very busy, and they are not going to be with you the entire time. So why are you there? Not to advise your wife to take some aspirin, but to provide for her emotional needs.

Just Be There

There is no person on earth who does not find some comfort in knowing that they are not going through an ordeal alone. I personally would feel more confident if I had a friend with me while confronting a hoodlum than I would if I had to confront him alone (preferably a big guy who is also a black belt). What many husbands fail to see is that their wives need them for emotional support. Just being there is a tremendous help.

Now if you're the husband and you only learn one thing from this article, this is it: During your entire lifetime, if you can learn to provide your wife with empathy when she is in distress, your relationship will achieve new heights. For me, the first few times the empathy was not from the heart, but, after a short amount of time, I really started to share my wife's feelings. And my comments became sincere. Maybe I wasn't at the level of Rabbi Aryeh Levine when he took his wife to the doctor and said, "My wife's foot is hurting us," but slowly I was getting there. One of the primary reasons women turn to other women for their problems is because other women know exactly what a woman needs to hear. Empathy.

Beside empathy, there are other things you can do to help your wife in labor. One of the pioneers who allowed husbands to join their wives in the delivery room was Dr. Robert Bradley. Dr. Bradley, who had grown up on a farm, noticed that all the farm animals gave birth in much the same way. They would lie down, relax, and let nature take its course. Dr. Bradley realized that contractions (which involve very thin muscles constantly working to contract the uterus) are less painful when a person is relaxed. Stress adds to the tension of muscles. In other words, if a woman's muscles are tight from stress and she is having muscle contractions, the pain is much more intense. Fear causes stress, which causes more pain during contractions.

Dr. Bradley developed the "Bradley Method" and was one of the first doctors to allow husbands (or other close relatives) into the delivery room. The results were astounding. There were significantly less medical interventions using this method than there were other existing methods (over 86 percent were spontaneous, unmedicated births). This goes to show you that a husband gets brownie points just for being there.

Knowledge, Knowledge, Knowledge

The fear and tension can be reduced for both husband and wife if they understand what is happening to a woman in childbirth. People who don't know what to expect often get panicky, and panicky people have a lot of fear and stress, unfortunately resulting in a more painful childbirth experience.

Some important things you should know are that pain is part of the process, and different women experience pain differently. The number of contractions a woman will have is finite, and every contraction brings her that much closer to having a baby.

Now, if you're at the hospital anyway, there is a lot you can do besides being an educated lump on a log. Labor can take a long time. My wife's first labor lasted forty-eight hours, start to finish. Despite having taken a Lamaze course, I didn't know what I was doing, and I was standing by her side for a good twelve of those hours. Most women do not want to deal with a husband who behaves like a chicken without a head when they are in labor. I cannot stress enough that knowledge is a good thing. Knowing what to say and what not to say can go a long way toward helping her, too. I will give a few examples later on.

Initial Stages

In the beginning stages of labor, contractions are fifteen to twenty minutes apart. They may not be too painful. You can help your wife keep up her energy at this point by letting her sleep between contractions or bringing her water, etc. Asking her what's for dinner may not be the best course of action at this time. Some women have a need to clean up a mess when they see one. If your wife has started labor and she does not require you by her side, you might want to help her by doing those dishes in the sink or picking up your socks from the floor.

It's Getting Harder

When contractions are about three to five minutes apart, you should be heading towards the hospital (unless you were instructed by a professional to go earlier). Now the contractions hurt a lot (thank G-d, each one only lasts a minute). You might want to try and help your wife relax. This might include talking to her softly, closing the door so she can't hear the screaming person in the other room (this might be hospital staff), dimming the lights, or even calling a nurse or midwife to answer your wife's questions.

One illusion I was under at our first birth was that a nurse or midwife was always going to be with us during the labor. I didn't realize that I would have to keep calling her to come to our room. So, having no one else, yours truly had to help his wife get through each contraction.

You might want to look at a fetal monitor and tell your wife that the contraction is over its peak, and it should be getting less painful. It's better not to make light of it, or tell your wife that "it's only one minute, after all." As Einstein proved, a minute undergoing root canal is not the same length as a minute at Disney World. And although I normally try to use humor to relieve stress, I learned the hard way that laughter adds muscle tension and makes contractions a lot more painful.

Talking should also be kept to a minimum; stick to key phrases like "You've come so far," or "Just finish this one contraction," "You're close to the end," or "It's almost over." (Repeat as needed.)

Finally...

At last the baby is born. Now is a good time to let your wife rest. In fact, you might want that to last for a few months. *What?!* you're thinking. Well, look at it this way. The baby will be getting up every few hours to feed. Now, I know very little about the Geneva Convention for the treatment of prisoners, but I do know that one of the rules is no sleep deprivation. It does terrible things to a person. Imagine this: every time your wife is just about to enter deep sleep, the baby wakes her up. If she is nursing, it is a 24/7 job (but much healthier for her and the baby).

I remember donating a pint of blood. They had a bed for me to lie down on and cookies and drinks for me afterwards. I give a pint of my fluids every six months and I get treated like a VIP. A nursing mother is donating her fluids eight to twelve times a day without any VIP treatment! I'm surprised nursing moms have any energy for anything else.

If the messy house doesn't bother you, it still bothers her; only she's too exhausted to do anything about it. Think about it — dishes, bathroom, floor, and laundry. If you can't do those things because you lack the skills, consider hiring someone or asking your mother-in-law to come help out.

If your wife is nursing, offer to bring her the baby, a cup of water, or the phone to return all the phone calls she missed from being so exhausted. Make up a little basket of things to bring her when she nurses (phone, towel, diaper, wipes, siddur, book, etc.). Don't worry, this will not last forever. But the easier you make it for her to recover, the faster she will recover.

Becoming a Dad

I was shocked that I didn't bond with my first child when he was born. As far as I was concerned, he was just a baby. I didn't realize that my wife had started the bonding process around five months prior, when she started feeling the baby kick. I didn't have this problem with my other children. Perhaps being a father for the first time took a while for me to get used to. One thing I do know is that holding the baby, changing his diapers and feeding him a bottle (when necessary) improved the bonding process. You can accomplish two things at once: speeding up your wife's recovery and bonding with your baby by changing and holding and helping take care of him.

The last thing I want to mention is to expect the tension level in the house to go way up for the first few months after a baby is born. You and your wife are sleep deprived, and you are both doing extra chores around the house. Some tips:
1. Put a note on the door that says, "Mother and baby resting."
2. Screen calls — talking can be exhausting.
3. If dishes are left in the sink or some laundry is around to fold when a close friend or family comes to visit and they offer to help, take them up on it.

4. The first couple of weeks people usually bring food. Accept everything! If it is too much, freeze what you can because by the third week, when there is little help and you are still tired, you will be glad to have the extra food.

Recognize that this tumult is a natural occurrence, and understand that this too has a time limit.

Most of my babies are teenagers now. It seems only yesterday that they were born. I see that although they did not always listen to my wife and me, they learned a lot from us. They observed our behavior towards others. They observed how we handled stress and how we dealt with the highs and lows of life. In fact, they use many of our mannerisms and they share many of the values we hold dear. They are also their own souls who, from birth, have plotted a direction for themselves. Raising children is very hard but fulfilling work. Being a father also let me understand why G-d, our Heavenly Father, is so compassionate, giving, and forgiving.

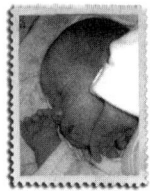

Out for Fresh Air

A father

J thought it would be easy. My wife, Shira, had taken a birth course and was well prepared. She wanted a natural birth — no interventions, pain medications, or episiotomy. She was willing to be flexible, depending on the progress of her labor. My role would be simple: say some *Tehillim*, give help when she needed it, and let the doula provide Shira with her "dream birth." It sounded ideal.

Then the big day arrived. We were having a nice evening out when Shira started having contractions. It was simple enough — there weren't any schedules to rearrange, and no one to call, except, of course, the doula.

After a few hours of watching Shira dance and hoola-hoop around our living room, it became difficult watching her try to cope. I wanted the doula to come, and she agreed it was time. Afterwards, she told me she had been ready for some fresh energy, a new face.

Susie came over with a bag full of equipment. She pulled out a rolling pin, aromatherapy oils, relaxation music, and other things. I could see she was worth hiring, as Shira felt more relaxed now that Susie was in charge.

It reminded me of coaching a team. Practice makes one more efficient. Doing this for one's own wife is a bit frightening, especially when a man has never seen his wife so vulnerable.

As the night wore on, we decided that the contractions were close enough and strong enough to go to the hospital. Susie also thought it was time to get the baby monitored. When we arrived, Shira was five centimeters open.

"Oh, no!" No way was she going to get to ten without an epidural. She was just about to get in the shower when I told her, "The doctor said it's okay to take an epidural if you need it."

"I don't want an epidural. I'm doing fine."

This is what she calls fine? I walked away.

Susie assured me that five centimeters is much more than halfway there. She reminded me that the cervix had to soften and ripen, which it had already done, and now the contractions were working on dilation and bringing the baby down.

Yeah, right. I went out for a coffee and some fresh air.

Shira came out of the shower in a sweat. When the next contraction came, I watched her pace and breathe while Susie pressed on some points on her lower back.

This was crazy. "You sure you don't want an epidural? My sister had one and said it worked great."

I guess it was time for a break, because Susie asked, "Did you daven yet?"

"Yes," I replied. "*Minchah gedolah.*"

"Maybe they need a minyan in the shul down the road."

I got the idea and went out for more fresh air. At that point, I decided to call my rabbi from across the country.

He had always guided me from the time I was young. "She can have an epidural if she needs to," was his reply.

Going back into the hospital, I found out that my wife was eight centimeters dilated. I said, "The rabbi said you can take an epidural."

At that, Shira said, "But I don't want an epidural! Why don't you take an epidural?"

I was a bit insulted, I must admit, but I got the idea.

Shira gave birth to a beautiful, healthy baby girl — with no epidural.

I decided to write this so other fathers could be prepared for the strength and self-sacrifice women show in giving birth to our children. Shira told me afterward that she wanted to tap into her inner strength and didn't want to be undermined by the staff...or even by me.

Maybe there are some husbands who are calmer, but the best thing some of us can do for our wives is to tell them how great they are doing, pray, and step out once in a while for some fresh air.

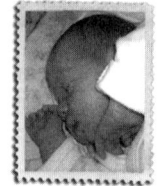

And You Thought You Were Tired?

Mr. Canada

Nine years ago, we were about to celebrate one of those Passovers that run into Shabbos. Some people may not mind the three-day *yom tov*, but some of us find it more difficult. In our particular situation, it was the lack of transportation and communication that made this birth more challenging.

This year we went away for Pesach. Seven children and a wife in week thirty-five were two good reasons to book a reservation at the Oppenheimer Hotel. It was located in a small town called the Fleishmans in the Catskill Mountains of New York. Not only was the price right, but it was homey enough for us to relax with our seven children in tow.

The fact that it was an eight-hour drive from our home in Canada didn't bother me too much. We would arrive the evening before Pesach, get a good night's sleep, and be well rested in time for the seder.

My wife, Gila, got the green light from her doctor. She had had no complications and had never delivered early, so I took out all kinds of insurance to cover the unexpected and made the booking.

The eight-hour drive went only a little less smoothly than a camel crossing the desert. Unlike the camel, we ran out of water. We also needed bathroom stops more often and changes of clothing from major accidents. Eleven, not eight, hours later, we arrived, truly ready for a vacation.

A couple of hours after we ate and settled in, I took a sleeping pill, ready for a good night's sleep. I wanted to wake up only when the morning sun called me to prayer. But just three hours into the night, I was awoken. "My waters broke," Gila announced. I was dreaming. I was sure I was dreaming.

"Are you sure?" I asked.

"Sure."

I was sick to my stomach.

One of the reasons we had picked Oppenheimer's was it was far from a big city. And I mean far. The closest city with a labor and delivery unit was a one-hour drive away. The problem was that they didn't have facilities for a preemie.

After contacting the emergency number of my insurance company, I was overwhelmed to discover that everything — including lost shoes — was covered; everything, that is, except birth! If Gila were to give birth in the U.S., it would set us back $10–15,000, not including the cost of infant care.

Since contractions had not yet begun, we made a decision to try to get back to Canada, where we had full medical coverage. The manager agreed to keep the five older kids, and we would take the two youngest. He would get his full payment, not to worry. They packed us food for the trip, including provisions for the holiday.

We decided to drive back on a route that passed major cities. That way, if things began, we could go into the closest major hospital to have the baby.

I drove with a newfound surge of energy that was certainly coming from somewhere beyond me. A half hour into the trip I realized I was driving in the wrong direction! One hour lost time, including the backtracking.

Binghamton, New York, was the first major city we passed. "Anything happening?" I asked.

"No, keep going," was the reply.

When we did stop for a bathroom break, I was nervous Gila would deliver then and there. There were still no contractions, but that didn't matter to me. And on we drove. It's amazing how anxiety can really keep a person going. At around eleven in the morning we got to the border — well, almost. The lines up ahead were so long you would think it was a holiday weekend. Actually, it was a holiday weekend. Now what? A border policeman. I told him the situation and we got his okay to drive down the emergency lane.

When we finally made it back to our neighborhood, the exhaustion set in. We dropped the kids at my parents' house and arrived home. My wife had a shower and I gathered together food and other items for a three-day hospital stay.

Once we arrived at the hospital, the doctor told us that my wife needed help to get the contractions going. My wife agreed that I should go home, have a shower, and get some sleep. I would call before *yom tov* came in to find out what was happening.

Shortly before candle lighting, things were just starting to move. Gila decided that I should stay home with the kids and she would manage without me. Neither of us was happy about the situation, but that's what we felt most comfortable doing.

On Pesach morning, I started out on the eight-mile walk. I was still tired, even after dozing on and off through the seder and an uninterrupted night's sleep.

When I arrived, I heard the whole story. By the time my wife was pushing, they realized it wasn't the head descending, but the rear. Breech. The doctor, looking nervous, said nothing was wrong. Then a second doctor said, "The baby is breech, but it looks like it'll come out naturally. It's too late for a cesarean anyway."

My wife was very nervous but delivered our baby, a son, soon after. By then, three doctors were in the room. "Can you imagine how much more nervous we would have been had we known all this in New York?" Gila commented.

After talking for some time, we realized we were hungry. I asked where the food was.

"I was so hungry, I finished it."

I walked back for the second seder, first sending our helper to bring food for my wife.

Gila also told me the following: While in the delivery room, she had received a message that our five-year-old daughter had hurt herself jumping off the stairs. She was taken to the hospital, but the staff needed parental permission before taking X-rays or performing any medical procedure. So now we had to wait three days to see how our daughter was. Well, G-d got us back to Canada in time, so we counted on Him to help our daughter, too.

Back at the hotel they treated our kids like royalty. They had such a great time I didn't think they would ever come home!

Appendix A

Resources for Dealing with Stillbirth or Neonatal Death

Below are addresses and phone numbers available for assistance in the unfortunate situation of having a stillbirth or neonatal death.

NEW YORK

Bikur Cholim Crisis Unit: 718-438-2020

Counterforce: 718-787-4412

Maimonides Hospital
Professional psychologist: 718-283-6000

Jewish Board of Family and Children Services
212-586-5770

Long Island University Hospital: 718-226-9210

Columbia Presbyterian Medical Center
Ob/Gyn: 212-326-5533

PHILADELPHIA

Shulamit (Shelly) Allon: 215-635-1984

ISRAEL

D'vora Grossbaum (Jerusalem): 02-651-8439

Merav Levi (Hebrew only): 052-425-5961

Tracy Prisman: 0545-751-995

ALEPH — The Israel Association for the Bereaved
A nonprofit organization of volunteers, started by and now continuing in memory of Michael Roskin, Ph.d. Lessa Roskin: 02-993-1649

Nechama
Organization for support and counseling during the bereavement period: 02-651-8319 or 02-573-4413

Appendix B

Resources for Dealing with Postpartum Depression

Below are organizations which offer assistance to women who are suffering from postpartum depression.

UNITED STATES

Jewish Family and Children's Service
Lakewood, N.J.: (732) 363-8010

Jewish Community Services for the Orthodox Woman
Lakewood, N.J.: (732) 730-1236

Monsey Family Medical Center
Monsey, N.Y.: (845) 352-6800

ISRAEL

NITZA — The Postpartum Support Network
02-5002824 or www.nitza.org

ENGLAND

Bikur Cholim D'Satmar
Postnatal support program providing practical support and assistance, including housecleaning, meals, medical referrals, and counseling: 208 8007575 or mail@bikurcholim.co.uk

Ezer Leyoldos
Caring for children and families in the Orthodox Jewish community with particular emphasis on ante and postnatal support: 208 8802488 or ezerleyoldos@hotmail.com

Glossary

Adar — The fifth month of the Jewish calendar.

baruch Hashem — Thank G-d.

brissim — Circumcisions.

chareidi — Ultra-Orthodox.

cholent — Traditional Sabbath stew cooked overnight on a covered fire.

Chol HaMo'ed — The intermediate days of the Passover and Sukkos holidays.

chuppah — Wedding ceremony.

Dayan — Judge.

Gan Eden — The Garden of Eden.

Gemara — Talmud.

gevald — An exclamation of dismay.

Hashem — G-d.

hashgachah peratis — Divine providence.

Havdalah — Ritual blessings recited at the termination of the Sabbath.

hishtadlus — Spiritual and physical effort.

Hodu laShem ki tov ki l'olam chasdo — Give thanks to G-d for He is good; for His kindness is everlasting.

Imeinu — Matriarch.

Imma — Mother.

kavanah — Intent.

kedushah — Holiness.

Kiddush — Sanctification of the Sabbath recited on Friday night over a cup of wine.

Klal Yisrael — The nation of Israel.

kvatterim — The couple that carries a baby into the synagogue for his circumcision.

Mashiach — The Messiah.

Matzah brei — A traditional Jewish food made of matzah soaked in scrambled eggs and then fried.

mazal tov — Congratulations.

meidele — Little girl.

mezuzah (pl. *mezuzos*) — A scroll affixed to the right doorpost of every doorway in a Jewish home, containing the verses of the Shema.

mikveh — Ritual bath.

minchah gedolah — Afternoon prayers recited early in the afternoon.

motza'ei Shabbos — Saturday night.

neshamah — Jewish soul.

Parashas Emor — The Torah portion of *Emor*.

pasuk (pl. *pesukim*) — A sentence from the Bible or Scriptures.

pekel — A package, usually weighted.

Glossary

Pesach — Passover.

rav (pl. *rabbanim*) — Rabbi.

rebbetzin — The wife of a rabbi; a woman of spiritual stature.

Rosh HaShanah — The Jewish New Year.

sefarim — Jewish books.

segulah — Spiritual remedy.

Shabbos — The Sabbath.

shavua tov — A good week.

Shehechiyanu — A blessing of thanksgiving recited for reaching the present moment.

Shemoneh Esrei — The silent prayer recited three times a day.

shivah — The seven-day period of mourning following the death of a close relative.

shmatte — Rag.

siyatta diShmaya — Divine aid or intervention.

Tanta — Aunt.

Tatte — Father.

tefillah (pl. *tefillos*) — prayers.

Tefillas Chanah — The prayer of Chanah.

Tehillim — Psalms.

tikkun — Recitification.

tzedakah — Charity.

yeshivah — Torah academy.

yom tov — Jewish traditional festivals, usually associated with the three pilgrimage festivals.

zemiros — Songs for the Sabbath day.

Glossary of Medical Terms

amniotic fluid — Fluid surrounding the fetus contained in a balloon-type sac.

AROM — Artificial Rupture Of Membranes; i.e., waters breaking

aromatherapy — Aromatic oils used, in birth, primarily for massage and relaxation.

biophysical profile — A nonstress test using ultrasound to evaluate the quantity of amniotic fluid and condition of the fetus towards the end of pregnancy.

birthing pool — A pool used for water births.

breech presentation — Presentation in which buttocks or legs are nearest the cervical opening (3 percent of all births).

cervix — Mouth of the uterus.

cesarean section/birth — Birth of a fetus by an incision through the walls of the abdomen and uterus.

crowning — The stage of birth when the top of the fetal head

Glossary of Medical Terms

can be seen at the vaginal opening, before delivery.

D and C — Dilatation and Curettage, a procedure of scraping and collecting tissue from inside the uterus.

dilation — Stretching of the cervix to 10 centimeters for the baby to pass through.

doula — Professional labor assistant.

ectopic pregnancy — A pregnancy which occurs when the fertilized ovum implants outside the uterus.

EFM — Eletric Fetal Monitoring.

epidural — Type of regional anesthesia produced by an injection of a local anesthetic into the epidural space of the spinal column.

episiotomy — An incision made in the perineum to enlarge the vaginal opening at the time of delivery.

fetal monitor — External, or the more accurate internal, tracking of fetal heart rate and contractions.

forceps — A curved-blade stainless-steel instrument used to assist in delivery of fetus when intervention is necessary.

hoola-hoop — Circular hip rotation used in labor to help the baby descend.

Lamaze — A method of childbirth education focusing on pain management, imagery, and diversion.

lunge — A position used to open the pelvis for descent of baby.

Pitocin — The chemical (synthetic) form of the hormone oxytocin that is released from the posterior pituitary gland to stimulate uterine contraction. It provides harder, more frequent contractions.

placenta — A specialized vascular, disk-shaped organ (similar to the liver) for maternal-fetal oxygen, nutrients, and metabolic exchange.

Swiss antenatal method — Breathing and coping techniques developed by Esther Marilus, a childbirth educator living in Israel.

transition — The phase late in the first stage of labor in which a woman dilates from 8 to 10 centimeters.

transverse arrest — Presentation in which the fetus lies on the side, horizontally, within the uterus (1 percent occurs in all births, requiring a cesarean).

ultrasound — Use of high-frequency sound waves for a variety of obstetric diagnoses and scan of the fetus.

VBAC — The term used for Vaginal Birth After Cesarean.

waters breaking — Term used for when the amniotic fluid starts to leak or actrually burst, an indication that labor will probably start within twenty-four hours.

About the Author

Sarah Goldstein entered the field of childbirth personally over twenty-three years ago, with the birth of the first of her six children, and professionally over nine years ago, with the first of four doula courses. She is now a certified doula and doula trainer for DONA (Doulas of North America) and works actively as a natural childbirth advocate, promoting safer and more empowering birth experiences through organizing seminars, creating tapes ("Balancing *Hishtadlus* and *Bitachon* during Pregnancy" and "Growth through Childbirth," with Rebbetzin Yitti Neustadt), and writing. Her first book, *Special Delivery*, was published by Targum Press in 2004.

Sarah lives with her family in Jerusalem, where she juggles attending births, caring for her family, and other projects which continuously come to mind as her head sinks into her pillow each night.

Feedback or questions on any of the stories and information presented in this book may be sent to the author at emgee@netvision.net.il or 122/8 Astora Street, Jerusalem 97451, Israel.